The Marketing of Professional Services

Other titles in the McGraw-Hill European series in Management and Marketing

The Marketing of Professional Services

Aubrey Wilson
Managing Director, Industrial Market Research Limited

McGRAW-HILL Book Company (UK) Limited

London · New York · St Louis · San Francisco · Auckland
Bogotá · Düsseldorf · Johannesburg · Madrid · Mexico
Montreal · New Delhi · Panama · Paris · São Paulo · Singapore
Sydney · Tokyo · Toronto

Published by McGRAW-HILL Book Company (UK) Limited

MAIDENHEAD . BERKSHIRE . ENGLAND

07 094239 0

5678 A W & Co 7987

PRINTED AND BOUND IN GREAT BRITAIN

To JHW and CHW

Contents

Preface

Although for nearly two decades writers and teachers in the field of marketing have lamented the product orientation of industry, it has for the most part escaped them that their own work has suffered from the same narrow view, if on a different plane. While the literature of marketing has expanded at an unprecedented rate, with its philosophy, approach, methodology, functions, planning, control, and pay-off covered from every angle, it has been, almost without exception, related to the marketing of products and not to intangibles.

Services of all types are taking an increasing part of both organizational and personal budgets, but those engaged in service industries must of necessity lean heavily on product-marketing methods because of the lack of information on the marketing of services. This applies whether the services are professional, such as banking, consultancy, architecture, accountancy, or broking; industrial, such as contract maintenance, security, transport, or design; or consumer, such as tourism, entertainment, or personal care. All engaged in the sale of intangibles know, if only instinctively, that the marketing strategies and tactics for services are applied in a very different way from those for products.

The differences stem wholly from the total dissimilarities of the concepts underlying the marketing of services and the marketing of products. While service-marketing concepts have been isolated and described, their implications have not been studied or understood. This is particularly true of professional services, where the problem of lack of marketing expertise is often aggravated by the lack of marketing motivation.

The need to market services has never been more urgent. The Monopolies Commission report on restrictive practices in professional services came down heavily against many of the restraints imposed on marketing, but most particularly on advertising and some pricing practices. If, as is likely, the report results in legislation to prevent restrictive practices by professional associations, then many professions where marketing has been non-existent will be forced into the market place. Even the senior professions of medicine and law and the newer but nevertheless restricted professions of surveying and accountancy will be under a new competitive pressure. The same pattern will probably emerge as has developed in banking, where there has been a perceptible move forward in the last decade from a total disdain of marketing towards an acceptance and practice of marketing techniques.

If it is accepted, whether voluntarily or forced by the changing environment, that marketing is needed, it will rapidly become obvious that professional service people highly trained in their disciplines lack the opportunity and facilities for obtaining a better appreciation of the concepts and techniques of marketing their services. No longer are they operating in a world which automatically takes expert and professional advice at its face value. How do they communicate effectively with people who could use their services? How do they overcome objections to their authoritative but perhaps unwelcome advice? How do they sell their services?

The answers to these questions cannot be found in marketing books or in the content of marketing courses. There is, therefore, an urgent need to set out in detail the techniques for marketing the output of the services sectors of the economy as a whole—not just professional services. But the canvas is too broad to be adequately covered in one book and the differences between the marketing of consumer services, such as house repairs, and professional services, such as contract R & D, are too great to be joined together effectively.

Thus this book has been confined to the marketing of professional services. This sector is perhaps the most challenging and fascinating, since marketing is sometimes an activity upon which there is a professional anathema, is frequently regarded with disdain even when it is permitted, and is rarely practised with the enthusiasm, creativity, and sophistication to be found in the marketing of goods.

The genesis of the book was the need to understand precisely what factors in the marketing of services of a research agency had contributed to its success. 'What did we do right?' may be a cheerful interrogative, but the answer is no less vital than the disaster-oriented 'What did we do wrong?' A substantial piece of corporate introspection and an analysis in depth of successful and unsuccessful marketing efforts produced an outline understanding of the differences in approach and method between goods and services selling. The author was perhaps fortunate in having spent half his business life in marketing goods and the other half in marketing services, so that a standard of personal comparison existed which was supported by the experience gained in researching markets for many service companies.

The result of all these studies, however, showed a lack of cohesion—of an underlying linking theory—which would explain both the reasons for a different approach in the overall marketing and the individual functions. This missing piece of the jigsaw was finally provided by Warren Wittreich, whose work is acknowledged in this book and who identified the basic concept of professional service marketing. Wittreich unquestionably has opened the way for substantial studies of professional service marketing of which this book can only represent at best a small step forward. If, however, it sets the parameters for more elegant approaches, it will have succeeded in at least part of its purpose.

The book is intended to be a highly practical one. Having enunciated the underlying concepts, it concentrates on their meaning in the terms of the buying/selling interface and their implications for marketing of the complex buying processes involved in purchasing professional services. Consideration of the ways in which professional services are offered showed that the introduction of marketing into a field which hitherto relied essentially on the buyer seeking out the seller, has resulted in minimal knowledge of ways, and substantial lack of ability, to identify market opportunities. Thus, methods by which these opportunities can be recognized, manipulated, and exploited have been explained. Marketing strategies, tactics, planning, and control are all examined to establish precisely how they are or can be used in the professional service field. Some of the important individual functions involved in implementing strategy—personal selling, media advertising, public relations, direct mail, merchandising, and new service development—are considered in the context of the special and peculiar circumstances of professional service marketing. Finally, the most sensitive area of all in professional activity is examined—pricing.

While the lack of professionalism in marketing professional services has been deplored, a major contribution to this situation has been the lack of professionalism in buying services. If hardly any information exists on marketing professional services, then it is true to say none exists on buying professional services. It is too simple a solution to suggest that it is only necessary to reverse the marketing procedure to arrive at the buying situation. Thus, the book has sought to provide an insight into the intricacies of buying services and to link the efforts of the marketer with the task of the buyer. Just as the various studies on the purchasing of industrial and consumer goods have also been manuals for marketing personnel, the author hopes that this book on the marketing of professional services might make a useful contribution to the improvement of buying methods.

The innovation introduced in *The Assessment of Industrial Markets* has been continued in this book in that a series of checklists has been introduced where a step by step approach or summary of vital actions will assist the marketer in the activity to which it refers.

Most books on management subjects tend to have an air of unreality in that they concentrate on a single, albeit comprehensive, management activity and divorce it from the total activity of the company. This is inevitably true of marketing books which look at the firm's operations isolated from their corporate environment. It is only the efficient coordination of all business activities which can ensure continuous profitability, and it is dangerous to place emphasis on one aspect, such as marketing, to the exclusion of others. Thus, while the overriding plea is for the introduction of marketing thinking and marketing action in professional services, it should not be taken that marketing is the most important aspect in the company's mix of activities. Such a view would be as dangerous as it would be misleading. Professionalism in marketing to match the professionalism marketed will always ensure the correct balance.

Writing a book induces the full spectrum of human emotions: from love to hate, from bravery to cowardice, from hope to despondency. The pain of composition and correction is offset by the elation of problem-solving and accomplishment, and the resentment of criticism by the pleasure of being able to acknowledge the enormous help which is invariably given with such generosity by friends and colleagues. I have more people to thank for their assistance in enabling me to complete this book than any other I have written, perhaps because the subject is a relatively untouched one and their interests as great as my own.

The business I failed to obtain and the clients I lost have been as much a part of my education in marketing as the projects acquired and the accounts that were held. To them all equally I owe my greatest debt, for, in the absence of any other form of education in marketing professional services, they were my university and my examiners and awarded my qualification.

Individually, I want to acknowledge the work of Jeremy Fowler of Industrial Market Research Limited, who was present at the conception of this book and participated in the seminars which provided its genesis. His many suggestions for the ordering of the book and for rethinking some of its basic ideas, which through too close an association had become clearer to the author than to an audience, have contributed immensely to its readability. His meticulous editing has protected the readers from my conscious enthusiasm and unconscious biases.

I particularly want to thank Mrs Mary Griffin of Smiths Industries for her work on the manuscript which was out of all proportion to anything that friendship might justifiably demand. She read the book a number of times during its evolution and at its completion and her advocacy for some fundamental changes has resulted in many improvements. Her infinite patience in discussing the theories and techniques which have been described and testing them both against her own knowledge of marketing and, more importantly, her experience in buying professional services, was invaluable. Chapter 1 has particularly benefited from her expertise in classification and much of the material on new services development has been drawn from her work to which she freely gave me access.

Marie Costello who has typed so many of my books once more sorted out, made sense of, and re-presented the manuscript in an acceptable form and never failed to point out my over-use of favourite words and incompatibilities between this book and previous ones.

Finally, I again pay tribute to my colleagues both in Industrial Market Research Limited and Associated Business Programmes Limited—two very professional service companies—who assisted me with constructive and creative criticism and by relieving me of duties which enabled me to complete the book in a relatively short space of time.

In seeking to acknowledge the help and guidance of others, the risk inevitably exists that they will be held culpable for the faults of omission, commission, style, and concept when all they have sought to do is to remove the grosser errors. Thus, my recognition of their aid is intended only to indicate the extent of my debt to them and not to absolve myself from responsibility for that which has been written.

Aubrey Wilson

London
March 1972

Definition

A professional service is one purchased by industry and institutions from individuals and organizations, and is designed to improve the purchasing organization's performance or well-being and to reduce uncertainty by the application of skills derived from a formal and recognized body of knowledge, which may be interdisciplinary, and which provides criteria for the assessment of the results of the application of the service.

1

What is a professional service?

The definition on page xvi is specific to the subject of this book and has been adopted to enable the argument to focus on those activities which, at least from a commonsense point of view, are regarded as professional services but which are not purchased by individuals. It is, however, important that the definition should not be regarded either as contrived or arbitrary. It has been evolved from research into professional services and their markets and was modified as the book was written. This first chapter has been devoted to establishing the validity of the definition.

There is very little doubt that the question posed in the title of this chapter could provide a very fertile base for a long, theoretical discussion and for intense polemic dialogue which itself might occupy a whole book. The practical use of such discussion may appear to be of limited value, but acceptable definitions are important. For a start, it is as well for author and reader to ensure that they are communicating adequately and that the author is writing about the same thing as the reader believes he is studying. More important in a subject as nebulous, in every sense, as the provision of any type of intangible, a clear understanding must characterize the relationship of author and reader in so far as there is agreement on precisely what has and what has not been included in the range of services for discussion.

Just as those who market industrial products have learned much of their craft from the techniques for marketing consumer goods and in some cases gone beyond them to develop their own methods, so the marketers of one type of service may be able to benefit from the experiments, errors, and successes which have occurred in other types of services marketing. There can be no cross-fertilization or synergism unless practical groupings can be devised. Without this, examples only have a relevance to the areas from which they are drawn. Any discussion of marketing professional services, to be useful, must move from the specific to the generic, but not to the generality.

However, there is an even more practical and important consideration in seeking to devise usable definitions and classifications. This is that, if an adequate system of classification can be developed, it is possible to determine whether there is a common link between services within the classification and, then, between the classifications themselves. If such a link can be established, it becomes practical to develop marketing modules which may well fit every service in any particular category, and, thus, it would not be necessary for those marketing services to have to relearn the marketing process for each new service or activity.

This is not to suggest that a marketing-module approach is necessarily achievable, but only that if it is to be achieved then classifications must be developed as a priority requirement.

Definitions—official and unofficial—are examined in Appendix A and, as is shown, they do not provide a test against which any activity can be assessed and which will enable it to be classified as goods or services. It is useful, therefore, to start with a distinction made by Harry Greenfield,[1] in studies based on an earlier work by Simon Kuznetz,[2] in which Greenfield first distinguished between consumer services and producer services, and it is into the latter category that the definition adopted here for 'professional services' falls. Thus, he identifies consumer services as those used by households and individuals in their domestic capacity, and producer services as those used by industrial and institutional organizations. Consumer services have been defined as 'Expenditures by individuals not organizations which do not result in the acquisition of goods'[3] and traditionally include such items as personal care, well-being (housing and life insurance), domestic help, entertainment, and transportation. The definitions are capable of much further elaboration, but since they are used here only to distinguish consumer services from producer services, they will suffice.

Producer services are broadly defined as those intangibles which are purchased for organizational, not personal, consumption. But producer services are best examined from the point of view of what they seek to achieve. From this posture, they can be categorized accurately as follows:

- Equipment services, i.e., all services associated with installation, running, maintenance and repair of plant, accessories and operating equipment, tools, instruments, furnishings, and fittings.

[1] Harry Greenfield, *Manpower and the Growth of Producer Services*. Columbia U P (New York, 1966). Pp. 7–10.
[2] Simon Kuznetz, *Commodity Flow and Capital Formation*. Vol. 1. National Bureau of Economic Research (New York, 1938).
[3] Jacqueline Marrian, 'Marketing Characteristics of Industrial Goods and Buyers', *The Marketing of Industrial Products*, Aubrey Wilson, ed. Pan Books (London, 1972). P. 12.

- Facilitating services, i.e., all services offered to facilitate the productive operations of organizations including the provision of finance, storage, transport, promotion, and insurance.
- Advisory and consultative services, i.e., all services providing general or specific technical expertise and intelligence, including advice on the use and acquisition of resources, research, education, organization, and marketing.

Professional services, as defined for the purpose of this book, will be drawn from the last two categories only.

In the past, services have not been found to be amenable to any single all-embracing definition which is generally acceptable. It is not surprising, therefore, that a subsection such as 'professional services' has also largely escaped definition and wholly escaped agreement. Indeed, the problem appeared so intractable that after almost three years deliberation by the Monopolies Commission on the subject of professional services, they only produced the anticlimatic: 'We have not found it possible to define them precisely or to establish a definitive list of professions. We do not in any case think such a definition necessary'.[1]

Concepts of professionalism

Nevertheless, the Monopolies Commission did attempt, in the Appendix of their report, to provide a description of what comprises a profession,[2] and in so doing invoked ideas ranging in time from Francis Bacon to R H Tawney and beyond. The reader is thus left with a wide range of choices, for example: 'A profession is a higher-grade non-manual occupation; non-manual in this context implies that the intellectual or practical technique involved depends on a substantial theoretical discussion.' The Appendix does, however, provide some useful criteria for designating whether an activity may be regarded from a commonsense, if not a legalistic, viewpoint as a profession.

> The designation 'profession' is not a permanent monopoly of a few occupations . . . professional status is probably a dynamic quality (reacting to social and economic change) . . . an occupation does not have to be organized to become a profession . . . an organized occupation is not necessarily a profession . . . presence or absence of a code of professional conduct does not signify professional or non-professional status.

But the key suggestion which reduces all else to ashes is: 'to achieve professional status, the occupation must be subjectively and objectively recognized as a profession.' '*Say's Law*' clearly applies here: 'If I says I am a profession, I am a profession.'

[1] Monopolies Commission, *A Report on the General Effect on the Public Interest of Certain Restrictive Practices So Far As They Prevail in Relation to the Supply of Professional Services*. Part 1. 'The Report'. HMSO (London, 1970). Paras. 4 and 5.
[2] Ibid., part 2, 'The Appendices'. Pp. 29–34.

3

Judging by the list of occupations which offered evidence to the Commission's hearing, there is a high degree of accord with the final view that anything called a profession is a profession. From the Advertising Association at one alphabetical end to the Worshipful Company of Spectacle Makers at the other, and including everything from Remedial Gymnasts to the Institute of Journalists and the Society of Chiropodists, all are professions.[1]

Perhaps the best review of definitions of a profession has been given by F. A. R. Bennion,[2] who accepted that there could be a wide view, as typified by Carr-Saunders and Wilson: 'Any body of persons using a common technique who form an association the purpose of which is to test competence in the technique by means of examination,'[3] and his own, narrower, definition: 'Advisory services (including concomitant executive functions) in matters requiring expert intellectual knowledge and concerning the physical and mental health of an individual or body corporate are best provided by a private practitioner whose competence and integrity are vouched for by an independent body representative of such practitioners.'

Bennion identified six attributes of professionalism which are well worth restating:

1 Intellectual bias. An intellectual discipline capable of formulation on theoretical, if not academic, lines, requiring a good educational background and tested by examination.

2 Private practice. A foundation in private practice, so that the essential expertise and standards of the profession derive from meeting the needs of individual clients on a person to person basis, with remuneration in fees from individual clients rather than a salary or stipend from one source.

3 Advisory function. An advisory function, often coupled with an executive function in carrying out what has been advised, or doing ancillary work, such as supervising and negotiating, or managing; in the exercise of both functions full responsibility is taken by the person exercising them.

4 Tradition of services. An outlook which is essentially objective and disinterested, where the motive of making money is subordinated to serving the client in a manner not inconsistent with the public good.

5 Representative institute. One or more societies or institutes representing members of the profession, particularly those in private practice, and having the function of safeguarding and developing the expertise and standards of the profession.

6 Code of conduct. A code of professional ethics, laid down and enforced by the professional institute or institutes.

[1] Ibid., part 2, 'The Appendices'. Pp. 2–3.
[2] F. A. R. Bennion, *Professional Ethics*. Charles Knight (London, 1969).
[3] Ibid.

4

These characteristics, Bennion argues, identify a group of vocations or callings essentially different from others and of particular value and importance to the community. He terms them 'the consultant professions'. They are perhaps as arguable as any other definitions and, indeed, may be suspected of containing some element of special pleading, but they nevertheless provide new shades of meaning and implications.

Certainly, the definition adopted for this book breaches both the Carr-Saunders and Wilson and the Bennion definitions, and does so deliberately. Both definitions lean heavily on the existence and effectiveness of a controlling body for the profession. These bodies, now under attack by the Monopolies Commission, have in the past and will certainly in the future if they are permitted, hold back the practice of marketing in professional services. Adam Smith's dictum 'People of the same trades seldom meet together even for merriment and diversions but the conversation ends in a conspiracy against the public or in some contrivance to raise prices' may perhaps not be fairly applied to all professional associations, but certainly to the buyer of their members' services it is seen to apply.

The use of the term 'formal and recognized' in the definition on page xvi, as applied to a body of knowledge, might also start its own arguments. For example, the *Common Body of Knowledge*[1] of the American management consultancy profession is not universally recognized within America, and such a common body of knowledge is completely lacking in marketing, education and training, business broking, and many other activities. Nevertheless, standards of practice and methods of assessment often exist in a way they do not exist in non-professional services such as contract catering, car hire, and security services. This is not to say standards in these activities are lower, only that they are judged by different and sometimes more realistic or measurable criteria.

Having now to some extent clarified the distinction between consumer services and producer services, and so far as the latter are concerned, between professional and non-professional services, it is valuable to study the further classifications which are possible.

The major part of the history of attempts to frame classifications has been assigned to Appendix A, 'The Importance of Services in the Economy', because it has attraction and usefulness in the area of scholarship rather than for the practitioner whose needs this book aims in part to serve.

Contemporary explorations of the service sector of the economy have continued in an effort to seek more precise means of defining what a service comprises. Three of these more recent methods are worthy of examination, even though one of them destroys the single thread which runs through all classical and contemporary definitions: 'A service passes out of existence the same instant as it is performed.' These methods are concerned with conceptual

[1] *Common Body of Knowledge Required by Professional Management Consultants.* Association of Consulting Management Engineers (New York, 1957).

approaches to services and relate to their durability, tangibility, and commitment. Perhaps equally significant and certainly very useful approaches have also involved the concepts of essentiality and testability.

Concept of durability

Simon Kuznetz devised the classic scheme of commodities classification in 1938 based upon the concept of durability.[1] He divided all goods into durable, semidurable, and perishable, and allocated to each subdivision a timespan related to a stage of production in the sequence from unfinished raw materials to the finished product at 'destination'.

Starting from this basis, Harry Greenfield[2] classified services on a durability continuum, using the distinction he had developed between consumer services and producer services which was referred to earlier. The effect of this distinction is apparent from Figure 1.1, but the characteristics there identified are not intended to suggest that the timespans are other than arbitrary or

CLASSIFICATION	DURABILITY	EXAMPLE
Consumer services	Perishables (less than 6 months)	Cinema shows, hairdressing, laundry, sports events, removals
	Semidurable (6 months to 3 years)	Hire purchase, accountancy, employment agencies
	Durable (more than 3 years)	Education, defence, health, life insurance, house purchase
Producer services	Perishable (less than 6 months)	Plant maintenance, factoring, auctioneering, distribution, linen hire, services, travel, brokerage, computing
	Semidurable (6 months to 3 years)	Advertising, public relations, contract hire, executive search, architecture
	Durable (more than 3 years)	Management consultancy, contract R & D, equipment rental

Figure 1.1 Degree of durability

that the slotting of services into the matrix is either absolute or definitive. The purpose of the representation is to reduce alternatives rather than to produce a precise categorization.

The very blurred lines which distinguish the performance of a service from its outcome tend to complicate the designations, since it could be argued that there are few, if any, services where the outcome could not be said to be

[1] Simon Kunetz, op. cit.
[2] Harry Greenfield, op. cit. Pp. 7–16.

of a long-lasting nature. In Figure 1.1, services have been grouped on the basis of the actual activity involved.

The important point stressed by Greenfield is not the precision of the assessment of degree of durability, but the 'parallelism between goods and services and the fact that services can be analysed in terms which have heretofore been exclusively reserved for goods'.[1] The value to the economist in terms of more accurate national income accounting, in the study of demand cycles, and in the concept and measurement of capital formation and other new uses is obvious. The value in marketing terms is in removing, or at least reducing, the intellectual and psychological barriers to the use of *appropriate* goods marketing techniques for services.

The buyer of producer services may just as much make a durable investment as if he were buying plant or land. This will give a starting point for the examination of marketing professional services, since comparison can be made of such marketing with the marketing of anything which represents an investment for business purposes (but it must not be assumed for profits, since many services are non-profit-making by intention).

When it can be accepted that services are in fact 'stockable' (e.g., computer programmes and other data), there emerge immediately problems of obsolescence, postponability, logistics, and finance, none of which according to classical theory and much modern thinking can, in fact, occur with an intangible.

Thus, the recognition that services can be classed as durable to varying degrees broadens the marketing horizon and makes the conceptualization of the marketing strategies more readily achievable.

Concept of tangibility
But if services can be durable they can also have a degree of tangibility. They are not, as once again classical theory insists, totally intangible in all circumstances.

The essential utility of services is precisely the same as that of goods and derives from the satisfactions they yield to the purchaser. For all goods, a service element is inherent, even if it is only those services associated with getting the goods from producer to consumer, i.e., distributive services, or the service implicit in a quick and economic means of communication which lies in the telephone instrument. In the latter case, the service element can be produced, stored, and transported. However, to take a further example from Greenfield, the service involved in a haircut, which is inherent in the activity, cannot be produced, stored, or shipped.

Unravelling the service element in goods is not just an interesting economic exercise. From the standpoint of the economist, the basis for believing that services provide a stabilizing effect on the economy which is examined in detail in Appendix A, can only be sustained if both durability and tangibility

[1] Harry Greenfield, op. cit. P. 9.

of some services can be proved. For marketing personnel, it may indeed point the way to 'need' isolation, provide criteria for identifying the decision-makers, and give the critical factors involved in a purchase decision. All this is dealt with in greater detail later in the book.

It thus emerges from an analysis of tangibility that the closer the criteria conform to those for goods, the closer will be the marketing methods for both services and goods. The more intangible the service, the greater will be the difference in the marketing characteristics of the service.

Any division on the basis of tangibility must be arbitrary but, as with durability, it provides a starting point for further refining of the definitions. The implications of the concept of durability are perhaps best exemplified in the manner adopted for Figure 1.2.

CLASSIFICATION	PRODUCER SERVICES	CONSUMER SERVICES
Services providing pure intangibles	Security, communication systems, franchising, mergers and acquisitions, valuations	Museums, auctioneering, employment agencies, entertainment, education, travel services
Services providing added value to a tangible	Insurance, contract maintenance, engineering consultancy, advertising, packaging design	Laundrettes, repairs, personal care, insurance
Services that make available a tangible	Wholesaling, transport, warehousing, financial, services, architecture, factoring, contract R & D	Retailing, automatic vending, mail order, hire purchase, charities, mortgages

Figure 1.2. Degree of tangibility

Concept of commitment

Yet another method of classification warrants consideration, since every dimension introduced permits further refinements. To the concepts of durability and tangibility can be added the concept of commitment; that is, the extent to which a service involves a short-term, medium-term or long-term obligation.

The underlying notion in the concept of commitment is the idea that the guiding and priority principle is not the essentiality of what is being bought, but whether payment involved is avoidable and at what cost.

The distinction between fixed and compressible expenditure is a real one, but it must be accepted that, in the long run, all expenditures are changeable. In the medium and short term, some expenditures are clearly fixed or determinable by the seller, while others can be changed at the discretion of the buyer no matter how essential the spending category appears to be.

A further distinction is concerned with the timing of the payment and the degree to which it is fixed or can be postponed. Most usually the purchase of equipment can be postponed, but rent cannot, or if it is, it merely accumulates for a later period.

Taking the two categories together, the highest commitment category is that in which payments are fixed both in amount and timing, while the lowest commitment priority is spending which is fixed neither in amount nor timing.

The assumption of this classification is the fact that most purchasers—consumer and industrial—view their budgets as a unified problem in which choices and necessities span the whole spectrum of spending categories. In fact, priorities in spending vary according to the degree of need or necessity. For the affluent firm, the choice may indeed be between desire and preference rather than necessity.

Although consumer services provide many examples of all degrees of commitment, the bulk of services purchased by business and industry (which include professional services) have some duration. In general terms, those services bought by business and industry call more for the type of commitment associated with consumer hire purchase than with that involved in consumer personal care. A method of delineating commitment is shown in Figure 1.3.

CLASSIFICATION	PRODUCER SERVICES	CONSUMER SERVICES
Long-term commitments requiring regular expenditure of fixed amounts of money; failure to meet such obligations may result in loss substantially greater than the amount of the missed payment	Insurance, loans, mortgages, R & D, pension schemes	Life insurance, house purchase, private medical schemes, accident insurance
Either long-term or fixed commitments, but not both	Contract hire (vehicles, plant, office communication systems), contract catering, business education, factoring, management consultancy	Accommodation rental, hire purchase, equipment rental, repair and maintenance of consumer durables
Short-term, flexible commitments, where expenditure is often postponable, reducible, or can be eliminated	Contract maintenance, security services, training, advertising	Private education, cleaning, laundering, public transportation, repair, direct payment private medicine
Optional services that can be indefinitely postponed	Welfare schemes, microfilming, design consultancy	Recreation, travel, entertainment

Figure 1.3. Degree of commitment

The implications for the marketing of services inherent in the extent of commitment in which the buyer of services will be involved now become clear. Just as in the purchase of goods when the value of the order is high, negotiations tend to involve top management and perhaps to emanate from it, similarly the longer and the more rigid the commitment in which a service involves a firm, the more complex the decision-making tends to become and the higher the number of decision-makers involved. As with all the concepts studied, there are exceptions, but the generalization is largely applicable and valid. Thus, the degree of commitment will have a pervasive effect both on the way an oher of services is made and the marketing support required up to the moment of offer. In this respect, services will not differ markedly from goods except in so far as the degree of intangibility will add to the general problem of obtaining understanding of the offer and a belief in its benefits.[1]

Other concepts

It is possible to develop other meaningful concepts for classification which may make additional contributions to the understanding of the content and nature of services. Thus, the *concept of essentiality* follows logically from that of commitment: the degree of essentiality of purchase identifies the purchasing priorities of an organization on the basis of the extent to which a purchase is postponable. For example, for almost every firm, the purchase of telephone services is essential for its operation, while the existence of an in-plant training organization might be postponed indefinitely.

The *concept of testability* offers another useful grouping. The intangibility of services suggests, incorrectly, that they are not testable in a scientific sense. While this is true for services where results cannot be measured—entertainment, personal services, house rental in consumer services, and advertising and public relations in producer services—there are whole ranges of services where performance and the results of performances can be measured, under controlled conditions, with varying degrees of accuracy; for example, medicine, transportation, and repairs in consumer services, and production engineering, legal services, and security in producer services. The extent to which services are testable provides another valid comparison with goods marketing and ensures that comparisons have a basis in the similarity of characteristics of the items compared.

The concepts in relation to the definition

So far the discussion has embraced all types of services from minor, indeed miniscule, consumer services to the most complex and long-lasting of industrial services. It is now necessary to focus on the professional service element

[1] The author is indebted to Ely M Brandes, Palo Alto, Calif., author of the Stanford Research Institute's Long Range Planning Service report on *Consumer Services* (1963) for this view on commitment in expenditure.

as defined on page xvi, to check whether it has its place in the conceptual framework propounded.

In Figure 1.1, there are professional services in all three headings, *perishable, semidurable* and *durable* (computing, legal, public relations, advertising, consultancy, R & D).

In Figure 1.2, professional services appear in *pure intangibles, added value to a tangible* and *making available a tangible* (mergers and acquisitions, engineering consultancy, financial services, architectural services).

In Figure 1.3, professional services can be shown as *long-term, fixed commitments, long-term or fixed, short-term, flexible,* and *optional* (insurance, business education, advertising, design consultancy).

Allowing always for the arbitrary nature of the criteria and thus for the slotting in of the services, it can be demonstrated that the concepts of durability, tangibility, and degree of commitment are as applicable to professional services as they are to any other class of services.

The remaining problem is to judge if the three major or other concepts can be brought together to create a series of modules all containing services with a strong common link between them. It is now common practice for companies following the Levitt dictum,[1] asking, 'What business are we in?', to seek a common link between a number of different activities. The example used by Levitt, that the railways were not in railways but transportation, showed the common link between air, land, and sea movement. A transport operator might see a common link between security (wages and bullion) transportation services, toxic waste disposal, and movement of works of art; each activity requires special vehicles which conventional transportation firms do not possess. But the three items exemplified also have another common thread: they all involve movement of materials and products which have a heavy downside risk in terms of loss or damage. In marketing terms, the 'plusses' of the firms in any or a combination of these fields would be expressed in terms of its special skills and resources.

However, a common link between totally disparate services may also provide a basis for developing a marketing approach, less through the uncovering of some aspect of the service which meets a similar requirement or satisfies a similar market than through observing the fundamentals of the marketing of each service and examining how far they can be applied to other services in the same module. At this moment, every problem in every service is still seen as totally different from all others.

Such an exercise requires that each service must first be categorized by the major characteristics of durability, tangibility, and commitment, and be appropriately located. Despite the fact, the classification criteria are admittedly arbitrary, the allocation of the service will rarely be clear-cut or absolute, and, indeed, a 'best fit' may be the most to be hoped for; the experiment is nevertheless worth the trial. For example, in Figure 1.4, advertising services

[1] Theodore Levitt, *Innovation in Marketing.* Pan Books (London, 1968). Pp. 39–66.

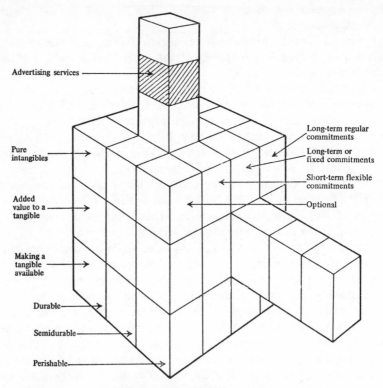

Figure 1.4. Classification system

have been allocated to the 'semidurable' (six months to three years) category. They are seen as a service providing 'added value to a tangible' and the commitment classification is 'short-term flexible'.

It will be found that executive search companies are categorized in a very similar way. The question then arises as to whether the more successful marketing methods adopted by advertising agencies and media salesmen can be adopted or adapted by executive search companies. Similarly, do architectural services, which are semi-durable, make a tangible available, and are a fixed commitment, have the same marketing characteristics as equipment rental, which also falls into the same categories? As heretical as it may sound, stripped of the professional reticence which surrounds them, could architectural services be marketed by the use of some of the successful aggressive techniques which have typified the operations of the leading equipment rental firms?

Thus, the categorizations can be used to identify services (and, indeed, goods) falling into any particular module and to examine the marketing tools and methods, and successes and failures so that comparisons can be made and adaptations examined to obtain the cross-fertilization which is so desirable.

2

Marketing and selling

While selling professional services is a well-known if not well-documented activity, the *marketing* of professional services, even those services which themselves offer marketing advice, is almost non-existent. It would seem that the differences between selling and marketing which were learned many years ago by the consumer goods producers, and more recently by industrial goods manufacturers, have yet to be appreciated and accepted by those concerned with the provision of professional services.

There are, of course, as many, if not more, definitions of marketing as there are of services, but they have in common that they tend to be arbitrary and not exclusive. The simplest definition and one which has aroused little controversy is: '*All those activities concerned with the purchase and sale of goods and services in industrial, institutional, and consumer markets and between organizational buyers and sellers.*'[1] The major function of marketing, it should be clear, is to present a company's offering in a way which will provide profit for the supplying firm while enabling prospective purchasers to perceive values for which they are willing to sacrifice alternative uses of their money.

The marketing process itself is relatively easily explained:

- development of marketing premises and targets;
- definition of services to be offered;
- development of marketing plan;
- resource allocation;
- data gathering;

[1] Aubrey Wilson, ed., *The Marketing of Industrial Products*. Pan Books (London, 1972). Introduction.

- situation analysis;
- operations
    creating and stimulating demand,
    locating buyers and sellers,
    negotiating price,
    provision of credit;
- monitoring.

Marketing process
To carry out the marketing process, the appropriate tools must be selected from a wide choice which includes:

- marketing research;
- personal selling;
- advertising;
- public relations (PR);
- merchandising techniques;
- pricing strategies;
- service range strategies;
- lead time exploitation;
- backing or support services;
- exhibitions and demonstrations;
- promotions;
- franchise dealings;
- financial incentives and aids;
- reciprocal trading;
- guarantees manipulation.

It can be seen that the emphasis is away from logistics. The functions of transportation, storage, processing, and packaging will, in most instances, be of little or no importance.

The combination of the process and activities which comprise marketing are inherent in the application of the marketing concept to professional service businesses. The marketing concept, however, is a philosophy, not a system of selling or an organizational structure. It is founded on the belief that profitable sales and satisfactory returns on investment can only be achieved by identifying, anticipating, and satisfying customers' needs and desires. It is an attitude of mind which places the customer at the very centre of a business activity and automatically orients a company towards its markets rather than towards its output, be this goods or services. It is a philosophy which rejects the proposition that output is an end in itself which, once produced to the satisfaction of the company, merely remains to be sold. 'Selling,' Theodore Levitt has pointed out, 'focuses on the needs of the seller, marketing on the needs of the buyer. Selling is preoccupied with the seller's needs to convert his product into cash; marketing with the ideas of satisfying the needs of the customer by means of the product and the whole cluster of things associated with creating, delivering and finally consuming it.'[1]

The important thing which has not yet been realized by those offering professional services is that the marketing concept is applicable to *all* business organizations (and even non-business ones such as trade and research associations, charities, religions, political parties, and causes), irrespective of the size or nature of the goods and services marketed. Differences in the type of output provided, the segments from which demand is derived or originates, the size and character of these markets, the purpose for which the output is required, and the route it takes from its producer to the ultimate consumer, do not remove the universal applicability of the marketing concept to business operations.

This doctrine is not invalidated by the fact that some professionals are prevented, by the terms of acceptance into the professional body and their conditions of practice, from 'selling' or 'advertising' their services. The restraints, legal and self-imposed, are restraints on methods, not restraints on marketing. Even the most rigid and punctilious of medical practitioners or barristers finds nothing objectionable in having their services 'referred' by existing patients or clients. The 'change of address' notice which announced the opening of a private practice by a medical consultant, and was sent to every GP who had ever referred a patient to him, may have been dispatched as a result of mixed motives. Indeed, the sender may have difficulty in identifying the marketing content of what is claimed to be purely communication of information: the conference attendances, learned papers, and TV appearances of medical practitioners and lawyers are not always motivated by the simple desire to impart knowledge. Are large or discreet window lettering, entrance signs, or site notice boards directed entirely to identifying the architect's location? Are the detailed stockbrokers' circulars designed solely for the purpose of providing information for investors?

Status and selling
It is, of course, all a matter of scale and approach. Since Jacob marketed his pottage to Esau, the exchange of goods and services between people has been characterized by the use of persuasive methods to convince one of the parties that the exchange, on whatever basis agreed, will provide satisfaction. Yet, to return to Levitt again, the question must be asked how often is it not just coincidental that the needs of the buyer are satisfied when the needs of the seller are also met? In a nation which enjoys buying so much, why is selling so unpopular? Buying is not possible without selling, yet people who enjoy buying often do not enjoy sellers. Certainly, the distaste and distrust of selling and salesmen are not things that were bred in primeval man on the

[1] Theodore Levitt, *Innovation in Marketing*. Pan Books (London, 1968). P. 51.

15

original day of creation; he has learned them somewhere. The chances are that opinion is based on costly experience.[1]

The important thing within the context of marketing professional services, however, is that the distaste for selling has rubbed off on the salesmen and back through them to all marketers in a great many service companies.

The reason is not difficult to see. The historical development of the salesman and the historical development of the professional have until recently been along widely divergent paths. The days of *caveat emptor* are not so long past, nor, indeed, are those of the pedlar and tallyman. There still hangs over all selling transactions a scarcely veiled suspicion that the salesman is attempting to obtain money from the unwary buyer by some trickery. This is because there is a natural and irremovable difference of interests between seller and buyer, based largely on the view that the seller is more expert, better informed on the subject of the sale, than the buyer who is an amateur. When the buyer is dissatisfied, he assumes that the seller deliberately withheld some facts that would have helped him make a wiser decision. Thus, he can hardly be criticized for exaggerating the extent of the duplicity by which he was cheated. Salesmen, to protect themselves from this dislike, have tended to hide behind any name other than salesman: 'sales engineer', 'representative', 'customer liaison manager'.

The development of the professional has been along a very different path. First, the achievement of legal recognition; second, the adherence to a self-imposed code of ethics; third, the recognition by society as a whole transcending national origin, political, social, or economic backgrounds. Few professions have achieved all three levels, but all activities which strive for professional status and recognition have these objectives consciously or unconsciously before them.[2]

The difficulty of establishing a bridge between selling (or even the slightly more acceptable 'marketing') becomes obvious from this perspective, yet it must be overcome if the marketing of professional services is to be accomplished. If marketing is to succeed, the marketing man must not only believe in his 'product' and what he is doing, but he must also satisfy an almost universal human need to be appreciated and achieve an acceptance that he makes a useful contribution to society. Without this motivation, professional services marketing will continue to take refuge behind real or pseudo-professional ethical barriers to justify the non- or even anti-marketing approach, while the deeper reasons remain happily hidden, since they are too uncomfortable to face.

It might all sound like a vast exaggeration to suggest that the corporate and individual ego is so riddled with doubt that it cannot perform effectively. Certainly, some professions are not known for their humility—doctors,

[1] Theodore Levitt, op. cit. P. 12.
[2] Warren J Wittreich, *Selling—A Prerequisite to Success as a Professional*. (A paper presented at a conference in Detroit, Mich., 8 January 1969.)

architects, lawyers—but these are the very professions where an anti-marketing attitude prevails most strongly. Thus, their members are not faced with the toxic combination of being involved in an inferior activity, which is how services are regarded compared to production (see Appendix A), as well as having to *sell*. These factors are the major forces behind the erection of barriers against the adoption of the marketing concept, and these barriers, so far as professional services are concerned, are all too often labelled 'professional practices'.

But there is nothing unprofessional in 'customer satisfaction engineering' which is what marketing is about. Business organizations depend on customer goodwill to survive and must learn how to sense and meet their needs effectively.

This truism applies in equal measure to professional services because, whether it is admitted or not, professional service firms must sell to survive.

> Whether the word 'selling' is one that we can savour or choke upon really makes very little difference, the 'burden of proof'—that responsibility for demonstrating that our credentials *really* mean something and will produce genuine benefits for the clients *constitutes* a selling proposition that we must recognize. In short if we can't *sell* our credentials in the sense of demonstrating that they stand for something far more substantial than the elegant initials after our name, then we are failures not only as salesmen but as professionals as well. As professionals possessing professional skills we still have not only the requirements, but the obligation of actively and energetically selling these skills. They won't sell themselves! We *have* to sell them. And if we have to sell them, it is better that we do so on a conscious explicit basis rather than on an unconscious, implicit, hit or miss basis.[1]

The case for selling professional services has not been better stated.

In the future, it will no longer be enough to regard the cursory PR campaign and the formal presentation as sufficient to maintain the firm's position and client list. No better example can be found than in marketing research. In the 1950s, the code of professional practice of the Market Research Society prohibited members of the Society from direct advertising and selling their services. One or two new companies decided they could exist without the benefit of the Society's approval and began to market their services aggressively and with skill. They had obtained a substantial foothold in the marketing research field before the Society relaxed its rules and allowed its members to compete. The conditions of market leadership had, however, been established by the 'pariah' firms, and it was they who dictated the climate of competition.

While it may be possible for professional organizations today to sit back and continue in the old manner, the moment one member breaks away from the pack, the situation will alter radically, unless such a break-away can be controlled by legislative means, as in medicine and law—something which is less and less likely to occur.

[1] Ibid.

In Britain, the situation is likely to change rapidly following the publication of the Monopolies Commission report on professional services[1] which called for a review of professional practices including restriction on entry, advertising, and price fixing. If under pressure the professional bodies accede to the changes required, then marketing will become a way of life in the professions much as it is in other industrial and consumer services.

What then, so far as professional services are concerned, does marketing involve which is not currently being practised? A nine point checklist gives the major areas where the differentiation between non-marketing and marketing, and marketing and selling, occurs.[2]

Steps in marketing

1 Generic service definition. For over a decade now business organizations have been aware of the dangers of too narrow a definition of their role. The classic examples are the railways seeing themselves only in rail transportation rather than all or any form of transportation which has already been quoted; film-makers identifying themselves as in the film business rather than entertainment; publishing companies as book suppliers, not information conglomerates. The same need for a broader definition of business is also obvious in services. Marketing research can no longer be regarded as a fact-finding process, it is essentially a market-oriented problem-solving technique; accountancy is developing from relatively simple auditing functions to embrace many aspects of company performance and management, including management consultancy and computer bureaux; finance institutions in the USA are moving towards one-stop financial services embracing real-estate development, investment banking, investment management, credit card operations, leasing services, and other related activities.[3] Thus, the first step in marketing is to develop an accurate, generic definition of the services to be offered.

2 Target group definition. The concomitant of a generic product definition is a wide market definition which it is then necessary to segment. Segmentation can be defined as the division of markets into homogeneous subsections having common key characteristics or requirements. The identification of these segments and their specific needs—technical and commercial—enables firms to concentrate their marketing resources on the sections of a market which offer the greatest profit potential or which meet other corporate criteria. Although segmentation strategies can be perceived in professional services, they are usually product-oriented, that is a market segment derives from a specialization in the firm, perhaps fortuitous, and not the other way round. Accurate group target definitions assure concentration of marketing resources.

[1] Monopolies Commission, *Professional Services.* HMSO (London, 1970).
[2] P Kotler and S J Levy, 'Broadening the Concept of Marketing', *Journal of Marketing* (Chicago, January 1969).
[3] E Netter, 'The Financial Services Industry', *Institutional Investor* (New York, January 1970).

3 Differentiated marketing. In approaching different market segments (there is no suggestion that a segmentation policy limits a firm to a single group), it is usually necessary to develop a differentiated marketing approach if the segmentation priorities are to have any meaning in practical terms. Not every segment of a market for a given service will respond to the same approach. Marketing insurance, for example, can be effectively carried out through the use of intermediaries of various sorts. It would be difficult to use intermediaries in management consultancy and virtually impossible with such services as loss adjusting, arbitration, and taxation consultancy. Banks may well be able to develop merchandising techniques for their services, but this is likely to be less appropriate for accountancy. The presentation of the service, the frequency of solicitation and/or exposure, the time and place of promotion, all require careful gearing to the target segments and their needs.

4 Customer behaviour and need analysis. In professional service markets knowledge of and attitudes to clients may be formed on impressionistic evidence. Folklore rather than fact can hinder the development of the service package offered, and of marketing segmentation criteria and differentiated appeals. Increasingly, firms recognize that customers' attitudes, activities, and requirements are not yielded without detailed and formal research. Industry and national archetypes are a poor guide for developing elegant marketing approaches. The provision of accurate and up to date information is a prior condition for successful marketing in every circumstance, and is perhaps one aspect of marketing which is rarely disputed. The need for data on clients, on the competition and on the environment, whether their collection is formal or informal, dominates every consideration of every aspect of the marketing plan and the application of every tool available.

5 Differential advantages. While service firms, because of the intangibility of their output, may have problems substantiating claims for their 'plusses', they tend to compound the problem by not relating these 'plusses' to their customer needs. As is pointed out in chapter 8, 'Identifying Market Opportunities', a 'plus' that has no value, actual or perceptual, to a customer is not a 'plus' at all. The premium promotion specialist on the advertising agency staff is just an overhead to the advertiser who does not use this method of advertising; the duplication of in-house facilities by trade associations could well be seen by some members as positive liabilities and not as a declaration of capability or comprehensive service. Every firm must consider what elements in its resources, capabilities, experience, or reputation will create special values in the minds of its customers.

6 Communication mix. The communication channels are diverse and the methods of reaching, explaining to, and convincing potential clients complex. Personal selling and PR are just two methods, press and direct mail two media, from perhaps a range of twenty obvious possibilities. Many methods and media are rejected by service companies as too brash, too costly, or too ineffectual, without any real consideration of their relationship to the company's services and markets. This unnatural shrinking of alternatives again reflects the distaste for marketing. Extreme examples drawn from the most strident parts of the consumer goods industry's communication mix are used to confirm the opinions of the inappropriateness of many techniques (e.g., stamp trading, coupons, gifts, and competitions). The rejection of a large number of the communication processes typifies and differentiates the professional service firm from the goods producing firm and from some parts of the consumer service industries. There is little doubt that the list of marketing tools given at the beginning of this chapter, particularly those relating to communication, will be largely dismissed as inappropriate, based on their face value and frequent overtones of consumer product marketing. However, even these have an applicability to the marketing of professional services, as later chapters illustrate.

7 Integrated marketing. Because of the wide range of marketing tools, coordination is necessary to ensure that their use is not self-cancelling. The fashion for the development of semi-autonomous marketing departments, still enshrined in many organization charts with advertising managers, service managers, PR managers, research managers, is dying because the need has been perceived for a single officer or department to have total responsibility for studying needs and undertaking the product or service development and communication programmes. Where marketing tends to be limited, the need for integration is neither pressing nor obvious. However, the adoption of a full marketing programme by professional service firms will bring with it the need to understand, develop, and implement a system of integrated marketing.

8 Continuous market feedback. The information-gathering process, formal or informal, is continuous in all firms. Most product businesses use their salesmen, research departments, outside research organizations, advertising agencies, and informal contacts to monitor changes in their environment and their own performance. Professional service companies tend to be more casual about collecting this vital information. The fact that there is no wholly accepted market-size figure for marketing research expenditure illustrates this point. In marketing, rather than selling, there is a continuous formal and structured market feedback. Information must be collected, integrated, and housed in a common data store drawn from externally and internally originated information which is required for the effective operation of the organization. However, it is vitally important that collection, integration, and storage should be purposeful, and that the information should be made available as needed and as appropriate to all levels of management.

9 Marketing audit. For a firm to remain profitable it must obtain periodic, reliable audits of its achievements, objectives, resources, opportunities, and threats. Basic business philosophies as well as important marketing aspects, such as those described and explored in this book, require a careful examination. Marketing audits, however, do tend to be used to monitor the course of the battle rather than to influence its outcome. As interesting as such an application may be, it is unlikely to add to the marketing capability of the company. The need to know when the change is required and the ability to make it before it is too late is vital for the continued existence of the firm.

Products versus services

The checklist of marketing activities which differentiate a sales as opposed to a marketing approach in professional services is, however, incomplete without an understanding of the concepts which underlie the differences in buying situations between the purchase of goods and services. The characteristics of goods and service buying are fundamentally different, and it is not surprising that there has been little appreciation of this fact, since professional marketing men have been able to give the providers of services very little help either in developing a sound body of theory or devising practical methods of marketing.

To begin with, the buying/selling interface in product and service marketing is differentiated by the most obvious fact that with tangible goods the actual product or a precise description of its physical and performance characteristics is usually available for evaluation, not the mixed cluster of activities —tangible and intangible—which comprises the spectrum of services. The buyer of computer bureau services can usually without difficulty assess the suitability of the hardware and software of the bureau; he cannot evaluate the quality of advice the bureau may give on the optimum approach to satisfy his needs, the efficiency of its personnel, the accuracy of the processing, and the reliability of delivery promises, until he actually experiences them. He observes, he applies his own judgement, and he makes his decision on the basis of what he expects to receive. This is part of the mystique involved in evaluating a service which does not apply in buying a typical product. Thus, in negotiating the purchase of a service, the buyer often feels as though he is putting his fate in the seller's hands.

Whereas buying a product usually involves choosing from a finite number of alternatives within well-defined categories, purchasing a service is often critically dependent upon which category of service is chosen. For example, buyers are not necessarily faced with a choice between consultancy services of the same type to meet a particular need. Should a firm seeking to enter a new market: engage a marketing researcher to examine its credibility and standing in the new field; retain a company acquisition specialist to advise and assist them buy their way into the market; engage an executive search firm to appoint personnel to develop a new company or division; or seek an advertising or PR agency to open the way for them to evolve into the product area?

These and others are decisions which can face just one category of buyers of services, and they take no account of the additional variables which are involved as soon as the categories of buyers are widened.

The end results of professional service activity (but not necessarily those of other services) are most frequently only identifiable in terms of intangible criteria, e.g., improved efficiency, skill, productivity, or well-being of the organization. Thus, to the problems of buying an intangible service at the outset must be added the problem of evaluating its successful performance and outcome at the end. This evaluation refers not only to the immediate impact of the performance on the buyer's business or activities, but also relates to the longevity of the effect it has produced. Unlike products, there can rarely be guarantees of results or warranties of life expectancy.

A useful summary,[1] reproduced in Figure 2.1, of the similarities and differences between goods and services has been attempted and highlights precisely where a product marketing technique might be applicable, where it will require some degree of modification, or where it is totally inappropriate. Although this classification refers to retail, not professional, services it is nevertheless highly relevant.

It can be seen that the similarities tend to outnumber the differences, but on a qualitative basis the differences may have more significance for marketing. If the examination is continued to other marketing activities and functions which were not considered in the article because they were not appropriate to retailing, the differences become even more fundamental. Most services are sold directly to the users of the service and middlemen have little if any role to play. Despite a degree of tangibility which may exist, the functions of storage and physical movement are not involved in service marketing to any extent. Guarantees of performance are infinitely more difficult to substantiate for a service than for goods—a situation which is further exacerbated by the fact that for many services there is no acceptable method of measurement.

Thus, in marketing services, particularly professional services, the product/ service differentiation will constrain the methods which can be used and require the creation of new methods or adaptation of old ones. Certainly, marketing activities to be effective will have to encompass in most circumstances the nine points enumerated earlier which differentiate the use of marketing in professional services and a purely selling or a passive approach.

The meaning of marketing

The explanation and examination of the marketing concept and the marketing process with which this chapter began occur in almost every book on marketing. Their implications have been set out far less frequently. It is under-

[1] R C Judd, 'Similarities or Differences in Product and Service Retailing', *Journal of Retailing* (New York, Winter 1968). P. 3.

CLASSIFICATION	SIMILARITIES	DIFFERENCES
1 *Product or service development*		
(a) Product or service development—incentives	Utilization of capacity problem	—
(b) Product or service development—sources of ideas	Market place as a source	—
(c) Product or service stages	Marketing programme	Patent unavalability for services
(d) Branding	Trade and service marks	—
(e) Packaging and labelling	—	Services lack use for packaging
(f) Warranty and service policy	—	Law of warranty appears inapplicable
2 *Sales effort*		
(a) Advertising	Objectives Institutions and media used	—
(b) Sales promotion	Use of printed promotion material Use of coupons	Lack of physical display in services No samples possible in services
(c) Sales management and selling	Use of contests and prizes Selling techniques	No demonstrations possible in services —
(d) Product differentiation	Service differentiation used to parallel product differentiation	—
3 *Pricing*		
(a) Price basis	Value Cost	— —
(b) Price management	Price variation principles	Services do not use discount structure generally

Figure 2.1. Product and service comparison

standable why this should be so, since at least one objective in this, as in other books, is to first gain an acceptance of the marketing approach to business. However, as Kotler and Levy have pointed out[1] modern marketing has two different meanings. One conjures up the terms 'selling', 'influencing', 'persuading'. Marketing is seen as a huge increasingly dangerous technology making it possible to induce persons to buy things, propositions, and causes they either do not want or which are bad for them. This is perhaps *The Hidden Persuader* syndrome.[2]

The other meaning of marketing is unfortunately weaker in the public mind; it is the concept of sensitive *serving and satisfying corporate and human*

[1] Kotler and Levy, op. cit.
[2] Vance Packard, *The Hidden Persuaders*. Longman (London, 1957).

needs. This was the great contribution of the marketing concept that was promulgated in the 1950s. The marketing concept holds that the problem of all business firms is to develop client or customer loyalties and satisfaction, and that the key to doing this is to focus on their needs. Perhaps the short run problem of firms is to persuade clients to buy existing services, but the long-run objective is clearly to create the services buyers need and to ensure that they are aware of them.

It is the second side of the marketing process that provides a useful concept for all organizations. Companies are formed to service the interests of particular groups. Many organizations lose sight of their original mandate and become self-serving, hypnotized by an easy success, dazzled by the sophistication of their techniques, misled by low key competition, and blinded by the belief in the imperishability of their services.

The choice for the professional service companies is not whether to market or not, but whether to do it poorly or well, and on this case the need for marketing of professional services is based.

3

The basic concepts in marketing professional services

By definition, the outcome of the application of professional services can have a profound effect on the performance and well-being of a company out of all proportion to the costs and fees involved in commissioning the service. Despite this gearing, the skills of buying professional services are as undeveloped as the skills of marketing them. The well-tried methods of purchasing and marketing goods have been found not to work, or to work inadequately when applied to many types of services, but particularly professional services. Reasons that this should be so have been indicated in the examination of the concepts of services in chapter 1, and also in the goods versus services comparisons in chapter 2, but the explanation is far from complete.

Whatever fundamental differences existed, they certainly failed to impress the pioneers of the marketing concept, since nowhere in marketing literature until the mid-1960s was anything other than lip service paid to the fact that an intangible does not share the same market and marketing characteristics as a tangible.

The only difference Converse, Huegy, and Mitchell[1] could see was that the emphasis in marketing was away from logistics. They merely described how the services were marketed without suggesting that the tools available were inadequate. Matthews, Buzzell, Levitt, and Frank,[2] many years later, while providing an unusual definition of services (activities, benefits, or satisfactions which are offered for sale), confine themselves to suggesting

[1] P D Converse, H W Huegy, and R V Mitchell, *Elements of Marketing*. 6th ed. Prentice-Hall (Englewood Cliffs, N J, 1958). Chapter 22.
[2] J B Matthews, R D Buzzell, T Levitt, and R E Frank, *Marketing: An Introductory Analysis*. McGraw-Hill (New York, 1964). P. 374.

that an analysis of customer needs, cost benefit studies, and 'product' adjustments are all that is required. But these are also requirements for product sales. Neither Leslie Rodger[1] nor Alexander, Cross, and Cunningham[2] make any reference to the marketing of services.

The notable exception in early marketing literature is McIver who, writing on marketing strictly from the advertising agency's viewpoint, recognized that professional service markets would respond to at least some modern formalized marketing methods. He could, however, see no difference between goods and service marketing. 'For an important part of the function of a banker or an insurance man (or indeed an architect or a lawyer) is to sell things; only where the grocer is selling goods to the community, the banker is selling services.'[3]

The lack of information, the lack of interest, and the lack of understanding of services and service marketing, reflect the inferior position of services in a product-oriented world.

However, in 1966, a considerable advance was made in the understanding of the concepts underlying professional services—an advance which was necessary before it was to become possible to adapt and develop marketing tools specifically for the purpose of professional service marketing. The work of Warren Wittreich must therefore be acknowledged as the breakthrough which service marketers had been looking for. Unfortunately, Wittreich's contribution did not make the same impact as Levitt's attack on the too narrow definitions of firms' activities. Although Wittreich's work was as important and fundamental as Levitt's, its implications were not understood.

In a *Harvard Business Review* article[4] Wittreich set out what he believed to be the basic concepts which underlie the differences between product and service buying and marketing. Unlike the definitions, classifications, and goods versus services distinctions, which describe but do not explain the observed phenomenon, Wittreich produced a new insight. He grouped these concepts under three headings:

1 Minimizing uncertainty. A professional service must make a direct contribution to reduction of the uncertainty involved in operating a business. The proper assessment of a service, unlike that of tangible goods, must take into account the impact of its performance on the client's business.

2 Understanding problems. A professional service must come directly to grips with the fundamental problems of the business purchasing that service. The

[1] Leslie Rodger, *Marketing in a Competitive Economy*. Associated Business Programmes (London, 1971).
[2] R S Alexander, J S Cross, and R M Cunningham, *Industrial Marketing*. Irwin (Homewood, Ill., 1956).
[3] C McIver, *Marketing*. Business Publications (London, 1959). P. 64.
[4] Warren J Wittreich, 'How to Buy/Sell Professional Services', *Harvard Business Review* (Cambridge, Mass., March/April 1966).

successful performance of the service, far more so than the successful manufacture of a product, depends on an understanding of the client's business.

3 Buying the professional. A professional service can only be purchased meaningfully from someone who is capable of rendering the service. Selling ability and personality by themselves are meaningless.

These approaches were explored by Wittreich in some depth in order to identify the practical consequences which emerge from them for marketing professional services.

The specific objectives of buyers and sellers may not always be aligned, but they are all encompassed by these concepts. There is a high degree of relationship between all three. The accomplishment of any one of them greatly aids the accomplishment of the others, but it is better to examine them separately and in isolation—first, in this chapter, from the viewpoint of the seller and then, in the following chapter, from the viewpoint of the user at the interface.

Sources of uncertainty

If the definition of a professional service (a professional service is one purchased by industry and institutions from individuals and organizations, and is designed to improve the purchasing organization's performance or well-being and to reduce uncertainty) is accepted, it can be seen that what the professional service organization really has to offer a client is not its skills and resources *per se*, but 'confidence', 'peace of mind', 'increased certainty in choice or risk situations', 'the reduction of uncertainty', or just simple 'hope'. How the reduction of uncertainty is achieved is, in a sense, almost irrelevant so long as the method is credible and commands the buyer's confidence. In short, regardless of terminology, tools, or techniques, what the professional service organization provides is the promise of introducing more certainty in a particular area in which the client feels unsure.

The implications for marketing services are as considerable as the realization some time ago that consumers do not buy goods entirely for their physical properties, but that they have important perceptual qualities which are not related to those properties. Services can also have perceptual qualities which endow them in the eyes of their users with more than the classical form, time, place, and possession utility, and includes all 'non-rational' satisfactions which a buyer receives.

The reduction of uncertainty may be the *raison d'être* of the purchase, but it may contain the intangible personal or corporate prestige factors. These themselves may make a contribution to reducing uncertainty, even if only as a placebo: among employees because they see actions being taken to remedy a situation; among shareholders because they approve the application of special expertise to their investment's activities; and among customers who may interpret it as a public affirmation of the intention of the firm to improve its performance.

There are many areas of uncertainty, the major ones being:

- Is a service needed?
- What service is needed?
- Who needs the service?
- Who should render the service?
- How should the service be rendered?

Their interdependence is manifest, but it is better to examine them separately.

The need for a service can be something which is realized by the purchasing organization as a result of its internal circumstances, operations, or environmental changes. It may, however, be the service provider who identifies the problem the service is needed to resolve. Creating awareness of the need for a service is a positive objective of professional service marketing. But whether the realization that the need for a service exists is self-identified or attention is drawn to it by someone or some organization other than the purchasing firm, an area of doubt will exist as to whether the need is real and urgent.

Some situations will provide a clear-cut answer. Continuing above-average staff losses, irregular manufacturing reject rates, low return on investment, and a high rate of new product failure, may well be indicators of a need for professional assistance. Foreshortened life cycles, a rising sales curve in a declining market, the rapid development of technically superior and different but competitive products may not point unequivocally to the need for assistance. Thus, uncertainty is often piled upon uncertainty at the outset. Is there a problem at all? And if there is, will a particular service solve it?

Given that the problem is defined accurately, the next area of doubt is precisely which service will resolve the problem. A falling sales curve could under different circumstances require the competence of an advertising or PR agency, a sales training organization, R & D facilities, cost accountancy, management consultants, or a 'commando' sales force. The would-be purchaser of services is faced with a bewildering array of alternative methods offered as a means of resolving his problem. Most of them will claim to be the alchemist stone which will transmute the base metal of the firm's present activities to the pure gold of high profitability. Deciding which service is applicable is itself a major source of uncertainty.

The problem of identifying who in the firm needs the service has its own complications and its own unsureness: the same falling sales might imply that it is the sales department and the sales manager who need help. But this decline in sales might well stem from product inadequacies which would call for the services of a consultant production engineer to reorganize production and assist the production manager; it might stem from bad logistics which would require an expert in distribution and transport to aid the

merchandise or transport managers; it could be the result of badly appor-
tioned sales territories which need to be reorganized by a marketing expert
called in to guide the marketing director; or the effect registered may be
outside the firm's control, some aspect of environmental change which a
sociologist or economist might probe and analyse and suggest to the board
how the threats imposed could be avoided and the opportunities exploited.
Thus, precisely where in the organization a service is needed is no more
clear-cut than the decision as to which service is needed.

Going a step further, if the decisions are taken as to whether a service is
needed, which service this is to be and in which part of the organization it
will be utilized, it still leaves the crucial choice of which, among a range of
competing firms, shall provide the service. How is the choice to be made?
How far can claims made in advance of the service being rendered be believed,
and what recourse will there be if the service company does not achieve the
objectives? This leads inevitably to the question of money well spent.

That a contract is given does not imply full and continuing confidence in
the ability of a company or individual to provide what is expected; on the
contrary, having committed themselves, the users are continuously, if sometimes unconsciously, looking for evidence to support their good judgement
in choosing that service company. Failure to find this evidence produces
dissatisfaction—none of which is turned inward, but all of which is directed
with growing vigour and venom at the service provider. Selling has only just
begun when the customer decides to use a service. The major sale comes in
delivering what is expected by the customer.

Because the real problem of identification of uncertainty is so hard to
uncover (by the buyer as well as the seller), the marketing of services requires
a special type of ability, empathy, and insight which most product marketers
possess to only a small extent.

If, however, the total problem of uncertainty is recognized as inherent in
every buying/selling relationship in professional services, and those involved
in the marketing of services are sensitized to sources of uncertainty, the first
important step has been taken to define clearly the considerations which
should apply in marketing services and the way in which marketing can
effectively encompass those considerations.

Understanding problems

The second concept refers essentially to the point of departure in determining
the ability of the professional service firm to deal with a given situation.
There are two possible approaches.

First, when a service organization has only a minimal understanding of
a client's problem either because it lacks generalized experience in the field
or because the client will not or cannot explain it, the emphasis by the
professional service firm is on extolling its own problem-solving abilities.
This is done by describing a generalized approach to most problems (per-

suasion by method), describing the abilities, experience and qualifications of key personnel in the firm (persuasion by personnel), or giving successful case histories (persuasion by success story). This is the *extrinsic* approach.[1]

Second, when the primary emphasis of the service organization is on coming to grips with a problem, it attempts to show its capability by concentrating on obtaining an understanding of the problem in depth. This is to enable it to generate both confidence and interest of the client in further discussions with the service firm. It then offers a first appraisal by further discussions or with detailed memorandum or project designs which reinforce the initial confidence. This is the *intrinsic* approach.

If marketing services is different from marketing goods, so, too, is buying services different from buying goods—a fact which few professional buyers will admit, even when buying for personal reasons. Frequently, buyers flatly resist the opportunity to buy on *intrinsic* considerations, that is by relating the offer to the satisfaction of real needs; and perhaps numbed by years of exposure to extrinsic selling—listening to the saga of 'I'm the greatest'—expect to be sold to on the basis of the extolling of the selling firm's abilities, experience, and resources.

Ideally, the would-be purchaser of services will approach the service company with a clear brief: 'We have a problem. These are all the facts of the situation. How do we resolve the problem?' This, alas, is a situation which occurs only infrequently.

The marketing man in a service firm is required to demonstrate the relevance of his service to the buyer's problems, but without any intimate knowledge of those problems. The burden of proof, as with selling products, is on the seller—a situation as inefficient as it is absurd.

If, however, it is considered that buying services is not dissimilar from buying people—and that is indeed what it is—then the analogy of comparison with the hiring of employees is a good one. When a prospective employee is interviewed, particularly at management level, every effort is made to inform him of the inner workings of the company. In buying people, the objective is invariably to obtain the services of the best person suited to the appointment. By comparison, value analysis has frequently and successfully demonstrated that in buying products 'second best' may be more economic and efficient. With people 'almost the best' is very much like almost passing an examination—laudable but nevertheless unsuccessful.

The principles which apply to the hiring of a person ought to apply to the purchase of services. They are not the principles that apply to the purchase of goods.

While prevailing practice is to avoid purchasing on intrinsic consideration, it is very much in the buyer's interest to buy on precisely these grounds. However, it would be unfair to suggest that service firms in fact take every oppor-

[1] Extrinsic selling is discussed in detail in chapter 10, 'Marketing Functions: Personal Selling'.

tunity to sell on intrinsic grounds. Indeed, the opposite is more often true—
even given the opportunity to discuss and understand a client's problem, the
seller still tries to sell on extrinsic grounds because this is where he feels
most confident. Many service firms tend to promote those services which
satisfy their own needs rather than those of the client. In manufacturing
industries, it is known simply as 'product-orientation', and that is just what
it is in a service business, too—a preoccupation with the 'product' and not
the customer.

Identifying the professional

The third concept involved in the buying and selling of professional services
is related to the professional's perception of himself, and how this is mani-
fested in dealing with the buyer, particularly in personal selling. Denigration
of selling and salesmen by others and by themselves, the brash image of
advertising and PR and other promotional techniques, the low status of
services, and the other factors referred to in both chapter 2 'Marketing and
Selling' and in Appendix A 'The Importance of Services in the Economy',
which affect attitudes of buyers and sellers, reveals itself in full when the
purchase of a professional's service is under consideration.

One thing is certain: accomplishing the necessary task of identifying precisely who is and who is not a true professional is very largely contingent on
the service company achieving the first two goals of understanding sources
of uncertainty and the client's problems. The provider of services who has
succeeded in reducing areas of uncertainty and of coming to grips with a
situation is by definition a true professional. However, since the achievement
of the first two goals is by no means wholly dependent upon the service
provider who may be hindered in his marketing professionalism by a total
lack of buying professionalism, it is as well to have other criteria for identification purposes. These may be summed up as follows:

- demonstrable knowledge and skill in the claimed area of competence;
- recognition of the limits of knowledge and skill.

While it is obvious that the demonstrable skill and knowledge will create
confidence, many professional service marketers fail to realize that the ability
to recognize the limits of their skill and knowledge also produces confidence.
Perhaps the particular inquiry or project will be forfeited, but the longer-run
opportunities remain for future exploitation. Certainly, a firm which has
turned down an inquiry as outside its area of competence will begin the next
inquiry which is within its competence with a considerable start over all
other competitors.

However, if every question the professional has to answer must be referred
to others within the firm ('I'll have to discuss that with our specialist'), this
identifies with professional salesmen—not the professional. Equally, the
all-purpose professional who claims for himself or his firm total competence

in every area of activity, and who is incapable of recognizing problems and situations beyond his capability, lacks credibility; nowhere is this better demonstrated than in year books which list companies offering services. Most entries of this type are paid for; thus the compilations tend to be little more than overdimensioned claims submitted by the advertisers. Export directories will show numbers of one-man concerns offering advisory services for any area of the world and for any product, in all of which claims are made for competence and experience. These are not professional firms by any definition.

Two basic types of salesmen can be identified:

The professional salesman. The professional salesman sees himself first and foremost as an individual with an outstanding ability to sell virtually anything. He perceives his role as limited to selling, and his personal qualities are the charisma of the salesman. He may, of course, have professional qualifications, but he does not view these as major strengths. He typically fails to bring them to bear on the substantive problems, but calls in the services of others to provide this. The professional salesman of breakfast cereals, ball-bearings, or insurance sells energetically, aggressively, and on extrinsic considerations. When he is forced into an intrinsic selling situation, he tends to adopt the set approaches of sales training courses which are virtually sales clichés, and he depends on others in the marketing or professional team whom he identifies as experts in the problem under review.

The professional who can sell. In contrast, the professional who also possesses sales ability perceives himself first and foremost as wholly competent in and committed to his profession. His ability to identify and isolate key factors of a problem provide his main business, intellectual interest, and job satisfaction. He seeks (sometimes to the detriment of the overall selling activity) to become personally involved in situations because he can do the actual work involved in the problem-solving. He knows either by instinct or training that the representative of the service organization must be capable of demonstrating a personal competence commensurate both with the competence of those to whom he is promoting and those to whom he is selling.

There is little doubt from this description that true professionals who can also sell are far more valuable to the company's clients than companies represented by professional salesmen.

Maturity in professional service marketing

Increasing maturity among professional service firms is bringing about a realization that the actual selling of professional services is only one part of the total marketing effort in which the company should be engaged. The significance of the concepts enunciated are that they have an all-pervasive influence on the form, method, and intensity of all marketing methods which are used, not just the selling.

The basic differences between goods and services, allowing for the degrees of tangibility, are so fundamental that it can be said with assurance that no marketing effort, however well-planned or elegant, will succeed unless it has recognized and allowed for the three basic concepts:

- minimizing uncertainty;
- identifying the problems;
- recognizing the professional.

All marketing efforts for professional service firms must be devised around these fundamentals. No apology is made for returning to them throughout the remainder of this book.

4

The buying/selling interface

Because so much marketing of professional services is passive, the problem of identifying market opportunities is never seen as a critical point in the whole marketing process. So long as it has been thought necessary for the first approach to be made by the firm seeking services, 'prospect' identification is not important. However, the moment the service company starts to market actively, the identification of potential buyers becomes crucial, and a method of grading inquiries an important aspect of marketing cost control.

But to understand the process for locating opportunities, it is necessary also to obtain an insight into the 'need' identification process within the customer company.

In professional service marketing, the key questions to which answers are required if the success of the marketing effort is to be ensured have been listed in the previous chapter, but are now re-examined. They are:

- Is a service needed?
- What service is needed?
- Who needs the service?
- How should the service be rendered?
- Who should render the service?

Is a service needed?
The recognition of the need for a service may come from several sources. It may be intuitive—that intangible and sometimes fleeting characteristic which distinguishes the successful entrepreneur and entrepreneural manager from others; it may stem from creative anticipation of the future; or from judgement based on the consideration of both historical and current factors.

Most usually the need is first recognized by the client himself. Here, three basic situations exist:

- The client has parts of a problem, but is not sure how to fit them together. The job of the service firm is to integrate them.
- The client thinks he has one problem when he really has another. The service firm must work towards a 'transfer' from the ostensible to the real problem.
- The client thinks he has a problem, but, in fact, there is none. The service firm must recognize this, and not seek to sell its services.

Of course, the identification of a need could come from the hoary old commercial traveller's approach of 'creating the need'. But *creating* a need which is not in reality a requirement is not marketing (it has been ingeniously defined as inventing a cure for which there is no known disease). The salesman's true role is better described as *identifying* prospective clients' needs.

This can be achieved in a number of ways. The phenomenon of 'multiple discovery' is well known to historians and scientists, and can have important implications in professional service markets. An identical problem will frequently emerge in totally unrelated areas. Its solution in one area can readily lead to the application of the problem-solving technique to other areas. A question of optimum pricing strategies in a multi-industry market for a particular product may indicate the existence of an identical problem, resolved or not, for other products in the same groups or industries, or the same product in other industries. In either circumstances, it may not have occurred to firms operating in the market that their pricing strategies require examination and revision because of the changing conditions which initiated the original demand.

Thus, in marketing professional services, the first task is to gain an understanding of prospective clients' businesses and to think with them and for them in the early identification of problems which match the capabilities of the service firm.

The reason why many professional organizations remain small may indeed be less because of the dependence of the firm on a limited number of people with the right mix of skills than upon dependence on individual flair for identifying need and an inability to communicate this flair to others in the company. Thus, the marketing arm of most professional service firms remains miniscule, and this, in turn, limits its output, growth, and development. Such a situation is unnecessary since need identification can be formalized as a systematic and structured process.

All who are involved in marketing are called upon to use their creative powers to the full. Nowhere is this more necessary than in developing a structured approach to need identification which can be met by professional services. Lateral thinking and the synectic approach which it is suggested in chapter 13, 'Service Strategy', can enhance skills in developing new services, are also applicable to need identification; the subject is, however, dealt with fully in chapter 8, 'Identifying Market Opportunities'.

What service is needed?

The identification of the need for a service does not necessarily imply that the type of service required is always clear-cut. Examples have already been given of varying interpretations of a service need as applied to the same situation. It is expecting too much of human beings to assume that any provider of services will not, in the first instance at least, attempt to see a service need in terms of his own services. However, an ethical and professional approach will ensure that if the best 'fit' is not one which the service provider can give, he will say so and even recommend alternatives. No matter how much professional service companies may know this and practise it, it may not be apparent to the seeker of services. Thus, a primary job in marketing professional services is to ensure that the potential client has faith that he will be advised objectively.

It is vital, therefore, that those who offer their professional services in situations where the need for a specific type of service is not unequivocal, must make their initial appraisal of the client problem on a totally open-minded basis. In circumstances of this type, an important part of the marketing task is to be sure the right service is offered, not only in terms of the company's professional expertise, but also within the full range of services (or indeed products) which may be available to meet the particular need even if the service firm itself cannot provide what is required.

Unfortunately, the situation is rarely as simple as this since the need for differing types of services may be concurrent at several levels of activity and management. For example, if expansion of manufacturing activities is being planned, is marketing research needed to validate market size and growth hypotheses? Should any expansion be based on present plant or should new plant be built? This may be the province of consulting and production engineers as well as accountants and other financial experts. If new plant is decided on, then where should it be located for optimum results? Here, the logistic and infrastructure experts may be needed. The questions are not mutually exclusive and, in fact, form a decision tree along which, at various points, different professional services may be needed to take the firm to the next point of decision.

Decisions are arrived at in a variety of ways, but the question which is posed in such a situation is: 'If management has been familiar with the professional services available for reducing the areas of uncertainty and resolving problems, would it have used such services?' The answer almost certainly is 'yes' which underlines a need for continuing communications between service providers and the customers they aspire to service.

This raises certain important implications for marketers of services. The successful projection of an image of competence in one field may rule the service company out in another. This is how it should be if the choice were, for example, between a firm with expertise in marine insurance to the exclusion of all else, and another whose areas of activity were limited to life insurance. However, a firm with an image and a substance of capability in mathematical modelling, linear programming, and computing sciences may not be considered in a situation in which a transportation and supply problem is involved because management cannot always make the transition necessary to relate mathematical modelling to their particular problem. The answer is again communication, but on an individual level.

Who needs the service?
The fact that different problems requiring different services exist simultaneously at different levels of decision-making has already been indicated. But given the ability to see this does not resolve the difficulty of who precisely needs the service; that is, who in the company will make the decision on: (a) which service will make a contribution and (b) which firm will be invited to provide the service.

It is not the PR officer who needs PR services, but his own 'internal' customers, such as the personnel manager or the chairman. It is not the head of management services who requires an ergonomicist, but the chief design engineer.

Although the personnel manager and the chief design engineer may claim no great knowledge of the techniques of the specialist they need, their role in the decision-making on the choice of service required and the firm to render it is vital.

The decision-making unit (DMU) in service purchasing is as difficult to reveal as in product purchasing. The DMU can be defined as a number of individuals who are participants in the decision-making process, who share common goals which the decision will help to achieve, and who also share the risks deriving from the decision. Thus, it embraces all those who specify, control, and purchase.[1]

There is now ample evidence from a large number of studies that typically three or more people will be involved in a decision to purchase a professional service, and it is not exceptional for as many as nine individuals to contribute towards both the decision to purchase a service and the selection of the service company.

Since the view is stubbornly held that the person designated in any particular situation as 'buyer' is the decision-maker, not surprisingly a very large number of sales calls and a substantial part of all promotion have been found to be routed to non-decision-makers or those who only contribute to the decision. Despite the fact that 'cold calling' is not common in professional service selling, an inordinately high number of calls are wasted as anyone

[1] Aubrey Wilson, *The Assessment of Industrial Markets.* Hutchinson (London, 1968). P.12 *et al.*

involved in marketing insurance, advertising, public relations, property, and architectural services will confirm.

In the same way information required by decision-makers is also frequently misrouted because of the wrong identification of those involved in the purchasing decisions. Technical data is given, for example, to decision-makers who are concerned only with the commercial aspects of the contract, and, of course, the reverse is also true.

The major questions for marketers of services are:

- Who initiates the inquiry?
- Who are the individuals involved in the decision-making process?
- On what basis will they make the decision about:
  (a) the service needed and (b) who shall render the service?
- What facts do they need to arrive at these decisions?

This information will not be yielded by waiting for it to appear, but must be sought out by research; not even when the approach is from the client side will the information be available automatically. Other than the fact that the inquirer, *prima facie*, may be one of the individuals involved in the decision-making process (but equally he may not be), all the questions still require answers. It is true, of course, that it is relatively simpler to obtain the necessary data when the initiative for the inquiry comes from the client side. However, only if the answers to the questions are available does it then become possible to plan and implement the marketing strategy and tactics.

How should the service be rendered?
The 'how' and the 'who' of services are closely interlinked. One will, to some extent, depend upon the other. But generalizations are useful at this stage. Clearly, in deciding how the service will be rendered, the purchaser is concerned not only with timing, but also with the way in which the service will affect day to day operations and, where applicable, how the arrival of service personnel will impact on his own staff. The long-term gains of the effect of the service could be easily nullified by the immediate adverse conditions created by the use of the professional service company. A new product search commencing with a corporate audit of strengths and weaknesses which, through tactlessness, ineptitude, or inexperience of the service company staff, may well be interpreted by senior management as a threat to their personal positions, may result in heavy loss of staff with disastrous results. Thus, the buyer sees the 'fit' of the service company to the purchasing company to be important.

During the execution of the service, there must be constant feedback of information on progress and results to the management of the purchasing company. This provides a stable operating arrangement. Service projects will sometimes change during their execution. Without good communication and feedback, the areas of uncertainty can widen and become more intense, and expectations may move out of line with reality. This leads to disappointment and frustration at the end of the project and often the problem the service was intended to resolve is not resolved.

Thus, the management of the purchasing company will need to know the type, frequency, and quality of the liaison which will be developed. This is particularly true where work on the buyer's premises is either inappropriate to the project, as in external training programmes, or intermittent, as in financial consultancy.

Just as the delivery of a product is not necessarily the end of the supplier's involvement, neither is the end of a service contract the end of the service company's involvement. The providers of professional services often have an open door through which to watch the developments stemming from the completion of the project. They rarely take advantage of this. The continued interest shown in the client's performance after the completion of an assignment clearly indicates the service company's confidence in its own work and demonstrates its commitment and sense of responsibility. It is one manifestation of its professionalism. It also provides opportunities for appraising new service needs. The 'hit and run' service provider is a menace to himself and his profession.

Once again, the buyer of services needs to feel, in advance, that in rendering the service it will be seen through to successful completion and interest will not die on handing over the last cheque. So important is the follow-on in professional services that many such companies are now building into their work, education, or training to leave the buying company with a capability for solving its own problems in the same field.

Nowhere is this better illustrated than in the introduction of corporate long-ranging planning into companies. This has most frequently been undertaken by management consultants who withdraw on completion of their work. Many firms which have installed corporate long-range planning systems then found that their own staffs were not sufficiently skilled or experienced to maintain the system which rapidly fell into disuse or was misused. Increasingly, a consultant's briefs when involved in corporate long-range planning projects is to assist firms to develop their own systems rather than to install one for them. In the process of this in-house development, the firm's own staff receive training and exposure which ensure that the planning system is an on-going process and is not dependent upon outside aid to maintain and adjust.

Who should render the service?

For the service company, this question is the key one. If need for a service has been properly revealed, correctness of the service offered has been proved, the identification of the part of the organization requiring the service and those who will decide on its implementation completed, and the method of rendering the service successfully explained, then the success of the offer should be assured. However, it is not. It is only at this last decision point that the combination of the basic concepts comes into play. In going through the buying process the purchaser, having arrived at the moment of decision on who shall provide the service, will choose on the basis of the company which appears to offer the greatest reduction of uncertainty, understands the problem most completely, and has demonstrated a high degree of professionalism. Thus, the correct handling of the first four questions is only to bring the professional service firm to the point at which the company is among those to be considered. Only in rare cases will all competition have eliminated itself at the first four hurdles. The main competitive battle commences at 'who'. To understand how the buyer arrives at this decision it is now necessary to reverse the process again and look at the marketing of professional services from the buyer's standpoint.

5

The selection of a
professional service company

In order to obtain an insight into precisely how an offer of professional services should be made, an appreciation of the selection and purchasing procedure used by the majority of firms is required. But, even before that, it is important to know why the service is being sought in the first place, if the content of the offer is to be relevant to the purchasing organization. With this information, it is possible to identify a sales opportunity, structure an offer which is apposite for the circumstances, and make a presentation which will be comprehensible, meaningful, and convincing to the potential buyer.

An immediate problem arises, however, in that the tendering or offer procedures for different types of professional services vary widely. Perhaps at one extreme is the advertising profession, whose offers or presentations are frequently on what can only be described as a grand scale, while at the other end of the spectrum are accountants who are rarely even asked to state a price for their services.

The procedures which are described in this chapter will apply to a very wide range of professional services, but obviously, under present legal or accepted practice, will have only marginal application to others. The warning has already been sounded, however, that these conditions may cease to apply to all but a very few professions in the future.

As will be shown in chapter 7, 'Implications for Marketing', the use of a professional service for almost all firms implies a high degree of innovation, if not in the actual introduction then in the implementation of the recommendations of the professional service firm. It is the degree of innovation which will govern the composition of the decision-making unit (DMU) and the respective roles and authority of its members. The degree of innovation is not, however, the only factor which will influence the composition of the DMU. Aside from expediency—such as who in the buying company may deliberately or fortuitously have knowledge of the area of expertise of the professionals, who may be available to liase with the professionals, or who has had past experience of the type of work they are doing—the reasons why the service is being sought in the first place will also have a strong influence on the group which will select the firm to provide the service.

Reasons for seeking a service

The degree of sophistication of a company's management or production processes will, to a large extent, contribute towards the situation in which a need for an outside professional service is perceived. Because business is a human not a mechanical activity, commitment to change or at least the consideration of change implied in calling in a professional service organization is often postponed until the 'right opportunity' occurs. This opportunity is all too often a disastrous alteration in the fortunes of the company which then obviates the need for a formal commitment—the company must now take some positive action if it is to survive. This is the situation in which the professional service companies, particularly services such as financial advice, management and production engineering and consultancy, advertising and PR, licence search, merger brokers, and 'head-hunters', are called on to act. It is clear that ideally before a company decides to employ a professional service company it should recognize the need for new sources of expertise, and this usually well in advance of the situation occurring which the professions are called upon to avert or exploit.

Aside from disaster or near-disaster situations, in which the professional is seen as a rescuer and when specific services, resources, and experience are not available inside a company in sufficient strength or numbers or at the appropriate time, the decision to use an outside service may be made under a number of varying circumstances. The major reasons for seeking outside professional services can be grouped under the following headings:

- the need for special skills required for a specific reason or intermittently;
- the nature of the problem—one-off, sporadic recurrence, long term;
- legal requirements (e.g., auditing);
- the need for total objectivity and freedom from internal pressures;
- lack of special resources such as laboratories, EDP equipment;
- cross-industry fertilization;
- anonymity or confidentiality (e.g., new product development, executive search, company acquisition).

It is obvious that the marketer of services requires an understanding of why an outside organization is needed to provide a professional service if he is to present the case for his own company in terms which are relevant for the situation. Emphasizing the availability of a tachistoscope testing facility, when the underlying requirement for the service is to ensure no internal leakage of information on a new advertising campaign, is to promote the wrong 'plus' in these specific circumstances.

The search for a professional service company

If the need for a service has been identified and generated by the company requiring it, rather than by a service firm, then the first steps in the process of deciding who is to provide the service will be for the firm to obtain information on all those companies which can, or which claim to be able to, satisfy the requirement for a service.

The actions of firms with previous experience in the use of a service company and those to whom it is a new experience will vary greatly at this point in the process of selection.

While both types of company may construct a list of 'possibles', from which the service organizations they consider unsuitable will be eliminated, it is highly likely that previous users of services will return to the companies which have satisfied them on other occasions. The very least they will do is include a previous and successful service company on the list they intend to select from.

Each stage of the selection procedure, which can be likened to an inverted triangle, will eliminate companies. The inverted base of the triangle may be large or small, depending on: the total number of firms which could be *included*, the extent of knowledge within the inquiring company both relating to suppliers of services and to their own needs, and the time available for the selection procedure.

Given that the 'prospect' has no previous contact or experience in the service area concerned, he will tend to seek and consider information on all possible suppliers of the service. Usual sources, of course, are business associates (hence the high referral rate of most established service companies), trade, business and research associations (e.g., the British Institute of Management, the Institution of Mechanical Engineers, and the Institute of Marketing), professional service associations (e.g., the Royal Institute of British Architects, the Law Society), directories, and year books.

There are many other sources of information which might well be invoked —universities, particularly those offering postexperience and postgraduate courses; chambers of commerce, especially those with overseas links, for example, the Anglo-American Chamber of Commerce, the Swedish Chamber of Commerce for the United Kingdom; commercial departments of overseas governments; consular offices; banks, again particularly those with foreign links; and trade papers.

It is not unknown, however, for seekers of services to examine a bibliography of the subject and then locate authors of books, articles, and learned papers, in order to commission their services either directly or through their companies. An examination of 'leads' of professional service firms shows that a very high proportion of all initial contacts which were client originated came through the publication of material related to the subject area, or to lectures and papers. This method of preparing a first screening list, although likely to be laborious and in some respects haphazard, has the advantage to the inquirer of giving a first impression of the capability of the individual and his firm, and his interest and experience in the professional area under consideration.

If at the end of this information-collection process, which, of course, can be a highly informal and unstructured one, the buying company feels it has too many names, it will commence a narrowing-down process. This is largely subjective ('Doesn't sound right, judging by the name', 'Address looks like a private house', 'Must be a one-man firm'). It might also involve a few inquiries to establish if the companies are known at all, or if they are mentioned spontaneously from a number of different sources. A company appearing in separate lists provided by, say, the Chartered Institute of Patent Agents, the British Institute of Management, the Institute of Marketing, a university, and a trade paper may prove to be a natural candidate for inclusion in the first screening list.

However, the more usual process, at least in respect of those firms which have not been eliminated on totally subjective grounds, is for information or the literature of the service firm to be requested or for an initial telephone conversation to take place to establish the scale, scope, and extent of the services and resources of the company. At this point, the prospective client is likely to be watching for the degree of specialization, client and job-listings, the appropriateness of the facilities for the problem under review, and professional recognition. Because, as yet, the service company can have little or no knowledge of the nature of the work to be undertaken, contact is on a generalized level. For the would-be buyer of a service, this has the inestimable advantage of making it possible to obtain factual data on the service company not coloured, deliberately or accidentally, by a claimed bias towards the problem area. The service company faced with the dilemma already referred to, of being asked to demonstrate their suitability for a project of which they have little knowledge, falls back on extrinsic selling techniques, that is selling the company, not what it can do for the client. Exaggeration and bias, even if not discounted at this stage, will not be particularly harmful since the inquiry is to obtain a first screening list, not to select the service company.

Detailed screening

Those firms which have succeeded in being included on the initial list of companies for consideration will then, in most circumstances, be subjected to more detailed screening. This may occur at the service company's office or the service company may be asked to visit the client. Although the former course is clearly the most advantageous to the would-be buyer of services, it is not, for all that, usually adopted. Many buyers of services feel that it is a matter of status for the seller to visit them and not they the seller; perhaps, once again, the buyer-seller relationship redolent of the Victorian pejorative of 'trade' still persists. If the prospect visits the service company, it will be possible, at least partly, to get the 'feel' of the company and to establish how far its claims are borne out by the physical evidence of its activities. An organization claiming to employ 30 architects might be expected to occupy more than 2 or 3 small rooms; a computer and computer terminal are not the same thing. Commercial status symbols are not necessarily indicative of top-quality work, but then neither is the use of very old machinery and furniture likely to invoke the feeling of a successful organization to any prospective purchaser of the company's services.

At this stage of the screening, the links of the company may be subject to the most careful scrutiny to establish its independence or if it is in any way controlled or influenced by other organizations. Cross-directorships are another important aspect which the client may check. The service company will be well aware that because one of their directors also sits on the board of other companies, it does not imply that clients' confidences are likely to be divulged. It is to be understood, however, that a prospective client might feel exposed or vulnerable on this point and may well eliminate a service company because of it.

Information will now certainly be sought on the qualifications and the experience of staff, for which some supporting evidence may be required. Claims regarding the possession of some physical resources, such as laboratories, audio-visual equipment, computers, information retrieval systems, and special purpose premises, will also be checked.

The service company may well be expected to permit the prospective client to tour their offices and to meet members of the professional staff of the company. The objection that a breach of confidence may ensue if this is allowed is not likely to carry very much weight and, in fact, may destroy confidence in the service company's claims at the very outset. While it is obvious that no proprietary information can be given in such conversations, a generalized discussion can provide important insights into the service company's skills and resources, and can be to the service company's advantage.

Buyers of services, both the skilled and the inexperienced, will usually use the detailed screening process to ask questions about the professional company's organization, background, and performance. How, for example, does the service company manned by economists deal with the need for expert scientific guidance in a particular subject area? If from internal staff, then the qualifications and experience of these experts will be requested; if external help is sought, from whom? What is to be the nature of the relationship between the service company and its own external suppliers of services?

The incidence of repeat business is another measure of a professional service company's satisfactory performance, and is one which the buying firm may link with the client list by checking on repeat business claims.

With the larger service firms another problem which arises for the prospective client, and which may need to be cleared at the detailed screening, is precisely *who* in the organization will undertake the project. It is a common criticism, and a justified one, that the top people in the service firm are seen during the selling process, after which a middle or junior man takes over. The problem of the service company in designating which staff will be assigned to projects when the details and the timing of the project are not known is very considerable, but the advantages to the buyer of knowing with whom they will deal are also considerable. This information removes the faceless aspect of the service organization and pins down where responsibility for the project will lie. Moreover, it ensures that if the project is successful and further work is commissioned, the same executive can be sought to undertake any new assignment. Professional service firms may have a continuous corporate life, but the individuals they employ change and there is no guarantee of consistently high standards merely because the same firm carries out the project. The skilled buyer of services, and often the less skilled, will seek to be satisfied on all these points before getting down to a discussion of the problem with the service company.

Assuming the would-be buyer is satisfied, the nature of the inquiry may now be discussed, or a further meeting may be called specifically for this purpose. It may have been delayed until this stage is reached because, unless the prospective client is reasonably certain a service firm is going to be asked to tender for the project, he may not wish to reveal the details of the inquiry since to do so will often mean that confidential information must be presented. The client will not want to talk in confidence with more firms than is necessary to enable a decision to be made as to which one will carry out the assignment.

It is when the subject of the inquiry is revealed that the professional service company can begin to show its expertise. While it is unreasonable to expect an immediate understanding in depth of a problem as soon as it is presented, if the subject is within the area of the service company's capability, it is possible for it to demonstrate a familiarity, at least with the terminology of the subject if not the problem itself. It is here that appropriate analogies are most useful, but the client firm may be more impressed by the quality of the questioning than by instant answers, potted assumptions, and glib solutions.

The offer
Whether the brief is given at the first or subsequent meetings or in correspondence, ultimately the service firm must make its offer. Because most professional services are complex and often esoteric, it would be unusual for this offer not to be in writing and to be most detailed. Today, few firms will accept a commitment that has not been spelt out in terms of content, time, cost, and yield of the proposed course of action.

Thus, whether weeks of work have gone into the preparation of the offer or whether it is a simple confirmation of a conversation, the proposal still has to convey to the prospective client all the things which might be said by the salesman were he present when the proposal was under consideration. It must be a package which meets the three basic concepts and must additionally communicate to all who read it the image which the service firm wishes to project. Unless the service provider has a clear idea what this is, then the offer document is unlikely to lend support to the image or the substance of the service company.

It is at this point that the client will decide whether the service company has really grasped the problem and if the solution it offers appears to be practical and to have a high possibility of succeeding. The offer will be the most tangible thing the buying company will have until the final results are available, and thus it becomes a measure or a symbol of whether value for money has and is being obtained. The offer document fulfils several purposes for the buyer:

- it is an insurance policy which enables him to check that he finally receives that which he has contracted for;
- it defines the services, facilities, and information to be supplied by the client and, thus, his non-financial commitments;
- it makes a considerable contribution to the reduction of uncertainty in the choice decision, both as regards the service chosen and the company selected to provide the service;
- it provides a first measure of the professionalism of the service firm by indicating how it has identified and come to grips with the problem, and how it rates its own capability in resolving the problem;
- it forms the legal basis for the contract.

A professional service proposal will contain many of the following elements:

- background—why the proposal has been prepared;
- statement of problem;
- project objectives;
- approach to be used;
- definitions adopted;
- scope of the project with, if necessary, detailed checklists of items to be included, or drawings and plans;
- methodology to be adopted;
- expected yield and its application in relation to the problem to be resolved;
- time;
- cost;
- staffing;
- conditions of contract.

Unless the proposal document is precise, unambiguous, detailed, and relatively unqualified, there is every likelihood that the inquiry will be dropped. Just as the professional who can sell will convey confidence in his approach, so the offer document must speak for the service firm with equal confidence; this is conveyed in the coverage, style, and presentation. 'Packaging' is always important and never more so than at this stage of the proceedings with the final hurdle just ahead.

It would be unusual if the client accepted a proposal without further discussion. In fact, the offer as it is presented becomes a chopping block. The buying company may require more details in one section, a facet of the service may be eliminated or divided between the sponsor's own staff and that of the service company. Whatever changes are introduced must be agreeable to both parties, otherwise the likelihood of clashes at the end of the contract, if not before, is very high.

Any revisions introduced and agreed at this stage will require writing into the final offer which will remain as a point of reference throughout the project. Because of the intangibility of services, the need for this point of reference is vital, although it is one which is not usually invoked until there is a dispute as to what the project is supposed to achieve or to contain, or how long it is to take or how much it is to cost.

The buyer of services will want to ensure that as many of these points as possible are covered by the terms of the offer and that it is as unequivocal as it can be made.

Finding a fit
The submission and agreement of the offer is not, however, the final act in the commissioning process. The client still has to decide, even if the service company is competent to undertake the project, whether it will be able to deal successfully with the buying company's staff (this appraisal may well be made before the offer is in fact submitted). Personal contact is the only way to assure the *rapport* essential for a satisfactory working relationship. Thus, at this point in the process, the client may wish to meet the professional personnel of the service company who are to be assigned to the project. These meetings will be less concerned with the service company's capability than with assessing its ability to work with client staff, its understanding of the problem, belief in its own offer, and to obtain reassurance on the internal and external empathy of the service company.

The would-be client will also want to know how much of the directors', partners', or senior executives' time will be devoted to the project, each individual's responsibilities, and what contingency arrangements exist for substitution in the event of service company staff leaving, falling ill, or otherwise becoming unavailable during the project.

When the client is satisfied as to the ethics, competence, and empathy of the service firm, there remains the final task of ensuring that the scheduling of the work is satisfactory and that everyone is perfectly clear what is to be done by whom and when. The prospective client will want the service company to devise a detailed work plan or provide a critical path analysis, so that the process and progress of the work is clearly defined and fits the requirements of the company. For example, a project which involved the design and installation of a new stock control system for a toy distributor required the work to be completed by mid-summer so that all the problems were removed and the system working properly by the time the seasonal rush built up for Christmas; failure to complete in time could have resulted in chaos and serious loss of business that might take years to recoup.

The client may also designate key dates for progress reports to be made. Generally he is less interested in the contents of these preliminary reports than in obtaining reassurance that work for which he is probably making progress payments is, in fact, proceeding. He, unlike the developer who has commissioned a contractor to erect a building, has no monthly certificates of progress nor the sight of the bricks, mortar, girders, and concrete rising above the ground as evidence of activity.

Go no-go

This description of the procedure usually adopted in buying a service is, of course, a generalization. Some stages may be omitted and some added, some contracted and others drawn out. A practical breakdown of the buying process has been made by the Marketing Science Institute in the United States[1] in what they have termed a 'buy phase'.

BUY PHASES

---

1 Anticipation or recognition of a problem (need) and a general solution
2 Determination of characteristics and quantity of needed item
3 Description of characteristics and quantity of needed item
4 Search for and qualification of potential sources
5 Acquisition and analysis of proposals
6 Evaluation of proposals and selection of supplier(s)
7 Selection of an order routine
8 Performance feedback and evaluation

Figure 5.1. The buy phases analytic framework for industrial buying situations

There is in the minds of most marketers confusion between the decision itself and the process which leads to it. Although some phases of the buying

[1] P J Robinson, C W Faris, and Y Wind, *Industrial Buying and Creative Marketing.* Allyn & Bacon (Boston, Mass., 1967). P. 14.

process illustrated in Figure 5.1 occur simultaneously, they do tend to be sequential. They show clearly that to view the buying process as a mechanistic moment of truth decision, which can be analysed separately from the problem content and the environment which gave rise to it, is unrealistic.

The buying decision, in fact, involves a sequence of incremental choices—the 'creeping commitment'. The likelihood that the 'creeping commitment' accurately describes the purchasing problem-solving process increases with:

- the importance of the buying situation to the purchasing company;
- the number of people involved in the buying decision;
- the reliance placed upon buying committees and similar arrangements for diffusing buying responsibility.

However, whichever method is used, the buyer of services will throughout be seeking to satisfy his urgent desire to minimize uncertainty in the buying decision as a prelude to minimizing uncertainty in the problem area which the buying decision is intended to resolve. He will, without question, be looking for reassurance that he has chosen the right service and the right organization to fulfil his needs and that his choice accurately reflects his ability to obtain value for his firm's money. If the buying sequence *and* all these underlying motivations are understood, much of the mystery and many of the apparent idiosyncrasies and aberrations encountered in buying professional services become explicable and the task of marketing is simplified.

The final decision, as in most purchasing decisions, is an odd amalgam of objective yardsticks and emotional expectancies. The objective yardsticks may well be price-to-yield ratio, time quoted, or guaranteed performance characteristics. 'Emotional expectancies' could be as different as increased status deriving from the use of a well-known professional service organization, the adoption of an exotic technique, a general feeling of confidence or being 'looked after', or just the comfort which stems from the self-knowledge of higher personal or corporate performance. The buyer examines the situation and then makes his decision on the basis of his perception of the situation and what he expects to receive.

6

Characteristics of buying situations

Markets and marketing are almost invariably studied from the perspective of the seller. This has led to the impression that the marketing activities which are most significant are those which occur when selling commences. This is incorrect. Marketing can never be wholly effective unless it is directed and implemented with a knowledge of the buying situation; a study of these situations must precede almost all other marketing efforts. The paradox exists that although purchasing is the end object of almost all marketing activities it is not seen as part of the marketing process. Moreover, and more significantly, because buying is not understood it is regarded as a relatively simple decision-making activity. Nothing could be further from the truth. Buying is a complex and dynamic activity. The schematic representation of the buying process in the previous chapter suggested that it is a complete series of inter-related decisions. This, however, is only one aspect of purchasing. Buying situations can also be distinguished by other characteristics which have important implications for marketing. A workable classification of buying situations has been devised, based on intensive examination of industrial buying procedures.[1] The buying situation has been found to group satisfactorily under some 12 headings which, allowing for common elements, has been further refined and reduced to the very manageable number of 3. This is summed up in Figure 6.1.

Extent of familiarity with problem
The major attribute of a new task (purchase) is that the buying company has no past experience on which to base its purchasing procedures or choice decisions.

[1] P J Robinson, *et al.*, *Industrial Buying and Creative Marketing*. Allyn & Bacon (Boston, Mass., 1967). Pp. 22–38.

TYPE OF BUYING SITUATION	NEWNESS OF PROBLEM	INFORMATION REQUIREMENTS	CONSIDERATION OF NEW ALTERNATIVES
New task (purchase)	High	Maximum	Important
Modified repurchase	Medium	Moderate	Limited
Repeat purchase (straight rebuy)	Low	Minimal	None

Figure 6.1. Distinguishing characteristics of buying situations

In a modified repurchase or repeat purchase, the buying organization can and does fall back on past experience of the situation and the suppliers of services. In such circumstances a new supplier has additional difficulties in securing a first contract. For example, in the supply of printing services to financial houses the major choice factors are invariably speed, accuracy, and the ability of the service company to work closely with the customer. Satisfactory experience on all counts makes it virtually impossible for a new supplier to obtain a contract since 'product', service, and personality meet the requirements of the customer and price is not significant. The downside risk is far too great to offset any likely economic advantages.

Information requirements
Information requirements will vary considerably, depending upon the newness of the situation, as is pointed out in the study *How British Industry Buys*.[1] Also: 'Differing awareness of important informational deficiencies causes buying situations to differ even when decision-makers have equally relevant previous buying experience. It is also assured that the informational requirements and information-seeking patterns will vary within each developing phase of the procurement process.'[2] The former study proved the need to obtain an understanding of the extent, detail, and class of information needed in each buying situation (so far as industrial products are concerned). To market services efficiently and to increase the chance of closing the sale, it is equally important that the marketing team should understand the informational needs of decision-making units and on a time continuum along the buying process.

Alternatives available
The problem of communication in relation to the would-be buyer of professional services identifying and recognizing all the alternatives available and the applicability of any particular service has been touched on in chapter 3, 'The Basic Concepts in Marketing Professional Services'. Buyers involved in

[1] *How British Industry Buys*. A study sponsored by the Institute of Marketing and Industrial Market Research Ltd. Hutchinson (London, 1967). This study is being up-dated and will be republished in 1972.

[2] P J Robinson, *et al.*, op. cit.

a straight repurchase have no need to consider the alternatives open to them. If the purchase is intended to solve a recurring problem which has been previously satisfactorily resolved by a particular service, serious consideration of alternatives is not involved, for example, the use of a Factor at predetermined times in response to the seasonality of a product and its demand.

In a modified repurchase situation, the information needs are not necessarily inconsiderable, but they are at least partly met from past experience.

In a totally new purchase, information requirements tend to be very great and sentient managements will go to considerable lengths to obtain all the data on which to base decisions regarding the choice of service and its provider.

The practical implications of the various classifications of buying situations need consideration if full benefit is to be derived from the understanding achieved of the buying processes.

As a first step, the marketer of professional services, either through personal knowledge of the buying organization or from research, needs to establish the category into which the buying situation falls and then to adopt the appropriate strategies. The incorrect identification, and, thus, the use of the wrong strategy, may effectively remove the service from the area of consideration by the buying organization. In a totally *new purchase* situation, the assumption by the service company that the buyer has knowledge and experience in the purchase subject will lead to a position in which inappropriate information inputs are given and the sales platform may well be based on a presumed level of sophistication of the buyer which does not in fact obtain. In such circumstances, the marketer of services may have succeeded in correctly identifying the buying company's problem, but will have failed to remove uncertainty; indeed, he may have increased it, thereby reducing the chances of a sale.

New purchase situation

The need for a new purchase may stem from changed conditions—environmental or internal—in the buying company. A franchise company, extending its operations to a foreign territory and having no experts on the legal situation of the country concerned, must seek the services of a lawyer able to advise them and resolve any problems relating to legislative factors. A franchise operation involving vehicle brake testing or silencer fitting on a drive-in/drive-out basis is, in the case of certain classifications of roads, dependent upon the appropriate planning authorities giving permission for access and egress to the premises. Information on local authorities' and central government's requirements in this respect is vital. The services of a legal adviser will be needed as part of a start-up operation will thus become a first professional service purchase in the context of the franchise to be initiated.

Changed environmental conditions resulting in a new purchase situation are to be found in insurance. There has been a growing volume of public and commercial cynicism which is typified by a well-known cartoon showing a startled man with the caption, 'What d'yer mean I'm not covered for that?' An attitude is also developing in which the insured uses every stratagem to obtain payment from the company on the grounds that insurance companies are equally sharp. Confronted with this situation and declining loyalty, some insurance companies decided that a 'facelift' was needed and an improved image had to be developed on the basis of 'no small print in our policies'. To appraise the strength with which attitudes were held, and the real basis for them, required the skills of pyschologists and motivational researchers; to devise a suitable image campaign, the resources and creativity of advertising agencies and PR consultants were used.

A new purchase may also occur where it is decided to substitute one service for another service or for a product. History provides an excellent illustration of a change in service occurring because of negative factors in the old service and alterations in the conditions in which the service was used. The rapacity of the goldsmiths of the City of London and their speculative propensities brought into being the Bank of England. The merchants' dislike of the gold-smiths and the fact that commercial development had reached a point where the advantages and significance of well-backed paper currency could be appreciated led to a new service emerging.

A situation in which a service replaced a product can be found in the post-war boom in leasing. Certainly, leasing companies, to judge by their success, have been able to convince many companies with liquidity and cashflow problems of the economy and efficiency of buying their leasing services rather than the products their services provide. In the consumer field, the dominance of television rental shows a similar substitution pattern.

Another circumstance which may trigger off a new-buy situation is the availability of a totally new service. To return to the banking example, no one could have purchased banking services in Great Britain before 1694 because they did not exist. Similarly, many of the professional services which are commonplace today were not available, nor was the sophistication of firms high enough to have made these services viable as recently as 25 years ago.

Whatever the reasons which have initiated the new-buy procedures the purchasing company will require information on many subjects: the approach of would-be suppliers to the problem to be solved, their capacity to handle the assignment, the capability within and available to the service firm, and its experience. Some of this data will be provided from internal sources and some sought or offered from external sources.

The modified repurchase situation
Modified repurchasing of a service will occur when changes develop along the buying continuum, that is, when circumstances make a regular rebuy inappropriate; an illustration of this is an environmental change which

occurred because of the decision of some Industrial Training Boards not to provide grants for short general courses in management training. The regular 'buyers' of these short courses, faced with meeting the full cost of participation, either ceased to send personnel or else demanded restructuring of the courses to meet the acceptance criteria of the Training Board. This situation, irrespective of its fundamental causes, induced a changed specification by the buyers of management training.

At the other end of the continuum a modified repurchase may be a manifestation of a new purchase situation becoming routinized. Demand for security services can be for a specific situation, for example, a particularly large volume of high-risk goods held at a factory because of a strike. This circumstance is one which can and does occur sporadically, so that the repurchase of the service on later occasions is no longer a new-buy position, but a modified rebuy in the light perhaps of minor variations in the nature of the problem. In such a situation, the goods might have been caught at the point of production, and in the rebuy situation at the docks or airport; the first circumstance may have been one in which large bulky items were involved which incorporates one type of risk, and the second small compact items which involves another type of security risk.

Between the two extremes of modified repurchasing occurring from changes in buyer specifications and from routinizing new buys, there are two intermediate conditions. These are where the marketers of services or the buyer seeks to achieve an improvement in an existing service or where an attempt is made to achieve greater economies in the purchase of a service.

The first of these intermediate situations is typified by merchant banks where, as attitudes to the provision of venture capital change, the services they offer become wider and their receptiveness to entering joint ventures or providing capital for what by merchant bank standards are totally non-traditional areas, becomes greater. This appropriately is typified by the investment excursions of the merchant banks into service industries on a scale which was not conceivable as recently as 1965. Thus, buyers of merchant banks' services could well find themselves in a repurchase situation arising from improved and extended services offered by the banks.

The second of the intermediate situations is where a company decides that the services it buys could be obtained more cheaply by 'value analysis' of the service—an activity which has largely escaped the attention of experts in this field. That this should be so is because cost-effectiveness of services is not always discernible nor calculable for many areas of activity. Value analysis applied to products can be very easily measured for cost-effectiveness, as the many tributes to the savings achieved have shown. For services such as, for example, the installation and operations of 'Management by Objectives' or 'Zero Defects' systems, the work of the service companies cannot easily be separated from other variables in the buying company and its environment.

However, an example of a modified repurchase position arising from the buying company seeking cost savings can be found in marketing research purchasing. Many buyers of research services have found they are paying for facilities they could carry out more cheaply internally. Thus, they have sought to buy only the components of a project they cannot themselves provide more efficiently. The research sponsor previously buying complete projects might ask the agency to undertake the field interviewing only, while the buying company handles the postal questionnaire through their own mail room, their computer analysis through their EDP department, and the price and catalogue collection through their sales force. The modified repurchase of services relates, in this instance, to the provision of a less complete service than the one previously supplied.

The circumstances which govern the reason for modified repurchases of services influence the marketing approach and condition the offer to be made.

Diagrammatically the situation can be illustrated thus:

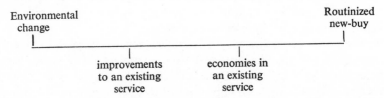

Figure 6.2. Modified repurchase continuum

Repeat purchase
A straight repurchase occurs when no changes are required or sought in the service previously rendered or the changes can be routinized in such a way as not to alter the conditions, yield, administration, and mechanics of the service.

A study to provide data on the viability of a new hotel in location A may require precisely the same techniques, information inputs, analysis, and interpretation as in location B. Although the configuration of the respective hotels may vary and their cost centres differ, the time involved in the studies and the methods to be used can make the purchase a straight repurchase.

However, a situation which has all the characteristics of a modified repurchase yet turns out to be a straight repurchase will occur when the buying company decides the cost and effort (break-costs)[1] involved in a modified repurchase outweigh the advantages to be obtained. It will then turn the purchase process into a straight rebuy.

Many services, despite their degree of intangibility and thus the difficulty in comparing repurchases, are nevertheless straight rebuys: accountancy

[1] Break-cost—costs associated with the change in supplier service, e.g., administrative, executive time spent in appraising, testing, and gearing-in a new supplier service.

and auditing, insurance, loss adjusting, property management, equipment hire, and the provision of some types of finance are examples. Figure 1.3 on page 9, which shows the degree of commitment, indicates where straight rebuys are likely to occur most frequently.

Innovative content of the service

The classifications, new purchase, modified repurchase, and repeat purchase, provide a predictive framework for developing marketing strategies and tactics, but they lack an important dimension. Obviously, there is a strong correlation between the criteria which are used to relate customer potential to the unique aspects of a service offered (the unique selling proposition)[1], and to a large extent this will govern the content of the offer. In exploiting unique combinations of 'plusses' with appeal to the individual prospective client, there is an implied and actual restraint on the content of the offer. However, whichever 'plusses' are selected as being meaningful and whichever classification is adopted for customers, it will still leave a large area of ignorance concerning how the buyers will react to the offer or how the buying decision will be made. The missing piece which enables the whole buying situation to be seen and understood is the *innovative content of the offer*, that is the degree of innovation, or change in practice or habit, which a particular decision to purchase will involve for the purchasing company.

Can a service which is being offered be fitted into the purchasing company's existing pattern of activity or rather, if bought, will it involve some change in that pattern? As has been shown, so long as sellers are offering well-established comparable services and are quoting roughly comparable terms, the buying decision is routine. When a buying company's pattern of behaviour has become established, however vital the services may be to it, there is no need for the intervention of higher management until the *status quo* is, or is about to be, disturbed.

> The purchaser's *status quo* can be disturbed by an offer containing implications of innovation, for instance a product which will involve changes in his production technology or in his product design. It can also be disturbed by commercial innovation as for instance a suggestion for reciprocal trading, a radical change in conditions of sale, or a really sharp price change. Any one of these things is likely to force consideration of change of habit pattern and so widen the range of people concerned in the purchasing decision. Whenever there is complication or disturbance of pattern the buying decision tends to be a diffused one. The less disturbance, the more the decision will be a buying department action with price as the dominant factor.[2]

Figure 6.3 illustrates the concept of innovation content. Clearly, the further to the left of the diagram, the more influential will be the buyer and the greater will be the influence of price. The further to the right of the innova-

---

[1] See chapter 8, 'Identifying Market Opportunities'.
[2] D Rowe and I Alexander, *Selling Industrial Products*. Hutchinson (London, 1968). P. 43.

tion scale the services are, the more functional officers and management levels will enter into the purchasing decision.

However, it is not enough for the seller to know the number and kind of decision-makers who will be involved. He must also consider the probable direction of the decision path. Will the decision be made, in principle, at the top and permeate down? Or will the proposal to purchase be initiated at some intermediate point for decision and sanction by higher levels or other departments?

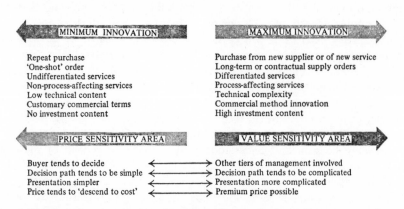

Figure 6.3. Innovative content of an offer *Adapted and reproduced by permission of David Rowe and Ivan Alexander from* Selling Industrial Products, *Hutchinson* (*London 1968*). *Page 44.*

Generally speaking, the higher the innovative content of an offer the more complicated becomes its presentation. Depending on the service, this increased complexity may either call for more negotiation of a commercial kind or for a more elaborate presentation of facts. In the case of professional services, such as design consultancy and R & D, precise and detailed presentations may have to be made, since here the services are not 'price' sensitive, but 'value' sensitive. Accordingly, the value offered to the buyer must be shown in a form which amounts to a value analysis made for him.

In extreme cases the presentation may involve documentation on alternative financing proposals, review of investment implications including case history material, and calculations showing possible cost savings for the buyer.

Nevertheless, the total bill to the buying company cannot be assessed solely from the price of the services offered. The buyers may have to incur other expenditure, such as own staff time, or they may enjoy savings of materials, process costs, or administration, or time or labour costs; they may gain additional safety or cleanliness, or silence or higher quality, or purity or accuracy, from the services.

Essentially, an understanding of the innovative content of the offer *to the buying company* and the implications of the innovation will provide a precise guide to the form and content the offer should take.

Using the categorizations
A knowledge of the category of purchase in terms of straight repurchase, modified repurchase, and new purchase gives very considerable guidance to the marketer both in identifying potential customers and in structuring the approach which is used. Additionally, with a knowledge of the reasons underlying the buying situation—for example, cost improvement in a modified rebuy situation—and an understanding of the buying sequences, the marketing task can be accurately identified and targeted and the route to its accomplishment plotted.

The strategic and tactical implications which stem from this knowledge, and which are related to the innovative content of the service so far as the purchasing company is concerned, now lead to consideration of the marketing approach.

7

Implications for marketing

An insight of the buying situation in any particular purchase helps towards structuring and focusing the marketing effort to meet the needs of that particular situation. It would be unwise, however, to assume that it is sufficient to identify any particular category of buying situation or service and then automatically apply a standard marketing approach or module. Because earlier chapters identified four generic classifications of services and three buying situations, it is not implied that a simple three by four matrix is all that is necessary to arrive at one correct approach. The use of classifications is to reduce the number of approaches and the components of the marketing mix and to avoid the grosser errors; it does not as yet provide a panacea for every marketing situation.

Knowledge of the buying situation is of the greatest importance in developing both the correct market approach—that is the method of communication and content of the offer—and equally vital, the correct timing. This chapter examines the implications for marketing of the various buying situations and suggests a number of appropriate approaches which can be adjusted to be compatible with both the service offered and the specific situation encountered.

Modified and straight repurchase

All repurchases have in common that the problem to be solved cannot, by definition, be a new one and thus no really new alternatives or few alternatives are likely to be considered by the buying company. The information needs of the buyers are likely to be more concerned with the identification of possible suppliers of the service and their availability, capability, and commercial terms. Figure 6.3, page 58, shows that, in total, information requirements are minimal.

Again by definition a straight repurchase situation has no innovative content, but it can be manipulated under certain circumstances to become a modified repurchase or a complete new purchase. Under either heading a small or considerable amount of innovation may be introduced.

The role of the marketer in a repurchase situation will, of course, differ depending upon whether he is attacking or defending. The 'plus' factors are all on the side of the 'sitting tenant': previous satisfactory supply, effective communications and relationships, a high position on the learning curve at the supplier/customer interface, an element of favourable break-cost, the downside risk of a new purchase, all often compare unfavourably with the advantages offered by a new supplier. Additionally, the general symptoms of buyer inertia and a tendency to minimize risk and enhance job security all favour the 'in' company.

Thus, for the existing supplier, the main effort is to maintain or improve that standard of performance which has made him the sitting tenant. Despite the preponderance of factors which favour him, he is nevertheless vulnerable unless he maintains active surveillance of both the competition and of changing dispositions in the customer company. Companies are composed of individuals, and individuals will not always, indeed, rarely do, act in a wholly rational manner even in an industrial purchasing *milieu*. Marketing does not cease to be important for the sitting tenant, although the mix of services offered and their content takes on a more important role than other marketing functions, such as advertising and PR. No company can afford to relax on the basis of past or current success when in most circumstances there are many competitors waiting to replace it at the first sign of weakness or failure.

For the 'out' supplier, the marketing approach is quite different. He must first isolate the reasons why the sitting tenant occupies that enviable position —performance, strategic reasons, personal relationships, reciprocal trading, break-cost—because these reasons will govern the content of the offer to be made. The out supplier can, of course, just wait until the sitting tenant fails to meet the standards established by the buying organization. Provided the out company's service is, indeed, regarded as a total substitute, then he will be considered *along with others* in the same category to be appointed as the in supplier.

Obviously, cultivation of the prospect by the potential supplier is an important and continuing process. A growing dissatisfaction with a current supplier must be appraised early if maximum advantage is to be taken of an opportunity to replace him. Nevertheless, this is a negative approach to marketing.

Positively, the forward-looking marketer of a service would be using the period to familiarize himself with the prospect's internal organization and communication systems, and any factors relating to the problems which the service is intended to resolve; to becoming acquainted with personnel in the decision-making unit and in generally preparing the ground for the day the opportunity to make an offer is afforded. He will also be seeking to establish whether his service can be endowed with a USP (unique selling proposition) of some type. If it can, then the marketing target is to reopen consideration of alternatives of which the modified service is one.

Such a situation may well arise with staff appointment service organizations. Almost all claim to test to some degree the competence of candidates and to check experience, qualifications, and background. A company offering all the services and also providing guidance on induction processes which, effectively conducted, can reduce staff losses by significant proportions, may well change a straight rebuy into a modified rebuy activity—a situation which must favour the new supplier and increase his opportunities for obtaining business. This additional service (or USP if no one else offers it) partly discounts the 'plus' of the 'sitting tenancy' of the existing supplier and makes the contest more even.

As in a new purchase situation, an environmental change may trigger off the opportunity for business. The marketer needs to be sensitive to any change, and its implications for buyers of services. The decision mentioned earlier of the Industrial Training Boards' refusal to give grants for some types of courses extended the opportunities for providers of those which did meet the Industrial Training Boards' criteria, a fact which needed to be communicated to companies currently using the external training and educational facilities. Alternatively, the availability as an in-plant arrangement of courses previously attended on a public basis offered some potential customers major economies which would offset the loss of the training grant. Again, this fact needed to be communicated.

The routinization of a new purchase situation also provides openings for business by turning such activities into modified rebuys. The annual renewal of many types of insurance policies usually only involves a reappraisal of the values of the items at risk or the circumstances insured against. Such a reappraisal can, however, be turned into a marketing opportunity by offering new 'packages' and new terms, not only for the insurance itself, but for services which might reduce the cost of insurance.

Where a modified repurchase occurs because the buying company is seeking improvements in a service, the emphasis, of course, goes on cost-effectiveness of the service bought. As will have become obvious from the concept of tangibility explained in chapter 1, and illustrated in Figure 1.2, 'Degree of Tangibility', page 8, cost-effectiveness of a service is always difficult, and in many instances impossible, to assess. Thus, the evaluation of the service may very well take place on the basis of price. This is particularly true in repurchase situations where price has a dominant role to play, since it is simpler to evaluate a service previously rendered than a new service.

Clearly, the identification of a repurchase situation is not always easy for the out supplier of services. Thus, it is necessary to maintain constant contact either personally or by some other promotional technique such as the interpersonal network. When any particular purchase of a service is being considered, the objective is to obtain 'instant recall' of the out supplier's name, so that he is considered for inclusion in any list of firms asked to prepare a quotation.

Appreciation of a new purchase situation

A factor which must be borne in mind in every new purchase situation, and which distinguishes it from both the straight and modified repurchase situations, is that uncertainties from all sources are numerous, and the risks inherent in the situation are far more pervasive than in the other two buying situations. The issues, as have already been indicated, are not only commercial and financial, but also psychological and personal.

In any buying situation, the buyers are subject to strong pressures which cause them to act with caution and to justify every decision taken. They will seek to minimize risks which are corporate in one sense and personal in another. This is the area of uncertainty the marketer must seek to remove and, therefore, the whole marketing effort must be geared to reducing uncertainty by the demonstration of an understanding of the problems to be solved and of the role and position of the decision-makers and by total professionalism.

The marketing approach which seeks to understand problems, reduce uncertainty, and demonstrate professionalism is the only one that can offer a consistent prospect of success. That is not to say that these approaches are unimportant in straight and modified repurchase situations; only that they are crucial in a new purchase situation. They meet the essential needs of all those involved in the buying process, although the way they are demonstrated by the service company will vary with the composition of the decision-making unit and the decision-making process.

Removing uncertainty

Because of the corporate and personal risks involved in a new buy situation, the removal or reduction of uncertainty is clearly a vital prerequisite for a successful sale. The sources of uncertainty listed in chapter 3, 'The Basic Concepts in Marketing Professional Services', indicate the approaches to be adopted for marketing under conditions of purchasing uncertainty. However, while uncertainty may stem from a totally new situation, it can also stem from loss of confidence in an existing or previous solution. The marketer has to decide, depending upon his offer, whether the major task is to restore confidence in the old solution or complete its demolition by the promotion of a new one.

In the techniques adopted for new product searches, the qualitative screening process[1] held sway for many years, but its deficiencies became increasingly obvious under the impact of the shortening life cycle of new products and

[1] *Developing a Product Strategy*. American Management Association (New York, 1959).

through a number of disastrous ventures based on the screening assessment of new possibilities. A new and successful diversification technique of product/market scope structuring emerged as a replacement for the old screening method, superseding it in terms of effectiveness, speed, accuracy, and cost,[1] although its protagonists continued to offer the old service for a considerable time, seeking to revive faith in the method. But the qualitative screening process contained in rudimentary form many elements of the more highly developed product/market scope-structuring methods, and the earlier confidence in the former could be transferred to the latter without being in any way contradictory.[2] This dual approach shortened the timespan in which confidence in the new method was built up, protected practitioners from the allegation of previously selling an ineffective service, and produced an overall synergism between the two techniques which led to the successful marketing of the product/market scope-structuring method. Uncertainties relating to the old method were removed and, at the same time, confidence in the new method was enhanced.

Understanding problems
In professional services competition in a new purchase situation is based on firms' reputations and capabilities rather than on price. Thus the marketing objective is to offer an improved solution to the buying company's problems. To do this means an early involvement in the buying decision when the marketing team can influence the specification or brief.

Since the buying process is in many respects a gradual elimination of alternatives, the importance of being among the companies originally considered and piloting the solution offered through the screening stages is, of course, vital. Although the chances of elimination are progressively decreased as the decision process progresses and alternatives are eliminated, the problem-solving approach must be flexible and responsive to the buying situation as it changes.

A large manufacturer of specialist packaging and printing machinery approached a marketing research company to assist it to obtain information inputs for a long-term diversification plan. Preliminary discussions revealed that there were, in fact, two problems: the original one posed of the company's long-term development, but also a second, more urgent one of falling sales of the existing product lines. The consultants put forward a proposal which involved two parallel projects, one of which was to be phased in two parts, to resolve the problems inherent in both the immediate and future situations. An examination of the suggested approach indicated to the packaging concern that their original order of priorities and time scale were not correct, and the consultancy company was rebriefed, this time along with

---

[1] *Planning a Diversification Strategy.* Industrial Market Research (London, 1970).
[2] Aubrey Wilson, *The Art and Practice of Marketing.* Hutchinson (London, 1971). Pp. 60–61.

two other companies, and invited to quote against the revised inquiry. The original consultants failed to obtain the project.

An analysis of the situation showed that the first consultants had, by stripping the problem to its essentials, helped the client to rethink his brief. This revised brief enabled the other consultants approached later to take advantage of the preliminary work which had been done, but left an impression with the client that the original consultants, having twice submitted proposals, had taken longer than their competitors to reach a suggested solution and to grasp the essentials of the problems. In fact, the first consultants were able to offer an improved solution because they had been able to influence the second specification. Having succeeded in this important marketing task they failed in the equally important communication task of explaining the nature of their contribution. Far from reducing uncertainty, they had increased it and thus, not surprisingly, found themselves eliminated.

Demonstration of professionalism
In a new purchase situation fraught with uncertainty, the demonstration of professionalism is especially important since in buying job security, which is fundamentally what all purchasers in industry seek, buyers are trying to purchase certainty and, in turn, certainty is more likely to emerge from a demonstration of professional capability. The prospect is listening for one message: what can this service, this individual, and the company he represents, DO FOR ME?

It has already been indicated that the truly professional approach to marketing a service will be based on the understanding of the buying company's problem. However, failing professionalism in buying, the seller is forced back to an extrinsic or semi-extrinsic selling role. The first sign of professionalism is to resist this necessity so far as it is possible to do so by concentrating the marketing effort on the substantive problem to be solved. However, it will be necessary on many occasions to sell extrinsically, and the mix of persuasion by method, persuasion by personnel, and persuasion by success story has to be applied with considerable skill and sensitivity during the buying process.

The overlap between extrinsic and intrinsic selling is considerable. As the buying processes move forward, so the emphasis in the selling approach changes. The professional salesman follows the extrinsic route to the moment of purchase; the professional who can sell switches from extrinsic to intrinsic selling as soon as the situation permits. The skill of the professional who can sell is his ability to use both approaches, phasing one out and the other in almost imperceptibly.

Marketing in a new purchase situation
The reasons which induce a new purchase situation must have an important bearing on the marketing approach to be adopted. Those reasons which stem from an environmental change provide opportunities for the service company

to appraise the existence and impact of the change often before the buying companies are themselves aware of these.

It was obvious in the United Kingdom that increased knowledge of the techniques of corporate planning would induce a new competitive pressure among firms to adopt formal corporate planning as one of the few ways to achieve a total competitive edge, rather than making small tactical gains in a given area or with a specific product.

A long-range planning service offered by an American organization in the early 1960s had a North American orientation, and activities in Europe were highly circumscribed by an insular approach. Changes in the emphasis in the service to a European orientation required a number of European clients, both to give the service credibility and to provide the necessary financial backing. A marketing plan was devised to introduce the service first in the United Kingdom where the language problem was minimal. Later, it was to be introduced into Continental Europe, based on a demonstration of the relevance of American experience in corporate planning, and offering the opportunity of improved performance through formal planning which in itself had no national connotation. A changing pattern of British industry, the wave of mergers, the increasing sophistication of management, and more intensive use of other management techniques were the environmental changes which provided the opportunity for the new service. The relevance of the long-range planning service to the emerging conditions had to be shown both by an intrinsic approach of relating the service to the corporate problems and posture of the prospective buying company, and extrinsically by emphasizing the advanced nature of the planning methods used, the wide range of skills and experience of the planning and research personnel who provided the service, and by stressing the success of the service among sentient managements in the United States.

Where a new purchase occurs because it substitutes an existing service or product, the role of the marketing team is once again to show that the problem the service is designed to solve will be solved more efficiently and with a greater degree of certainty. Here, however, the marketer may require more than just intense knowledge of his own service. He also needs to understand the substituted service or product in order to demonstrate the superiority of his service.

Microfilm services of various types provide a relevant example. The alternative to microfilming (whether in-house or agency) is to retain the documents concerned. To demonstrate the value of the service to a company, some simple financial calculations of space cost, retrieval cost, and security costs can be easily produced. What is not so simple to demonstrate and to be convincing about is how it is possible to overcome objections to reading documents on a cumbersome machine rather than in a location and at a time most convenient to users, as can be done with most documents, and also to counter the reaction against print-outs that lack the clarity of the original. Even more difficult to calculate is the cost of excessive print-outs to return the microfilm into a comparable state to the original documents, again to obtain the convenience of time and location. The marketing team need to understand the technical, commercial, and human situations in general terms and the conditions specific to the company contemplating the changeover.

While it is frequently the case that price is a matter of less concern in a new purchase situation, comparison will nevertheless be made where the new purchase is a substitution. Although past experience may not be relevant, a basis does exist for some type of comparison and this will certainly be made.

The third circumstance of a new purchase situation is the emergence of a totally new service. Here, the primary purpose of the marketing effort will be in the 'need identification' area, since without knowledge of the service (although perhaps with sensitivity to a situation which requires resolution) the potential user is not likely to express a requirement for the service, as such. The marketing team will have to be capable of assisting the purchasing company to express its need and then to re-express in the form of a new service to meet it.

Two other reasons may stimulate a new purchase situation, although they are equally applicable to a modified repurchase where modification is of an extensive nature. These are where confidence has been lost in the previous service as a means of resolving a problem or where a solution has become outdated.

An example has already been referred to in chapter 4, 'The Buying/Selling Interface', concerning corporate long-range planning consultancy. Over a period of time companies wishing to install planning systems found that, while elegant corporate planning schemes could be devised, implementation proved to be extremely difficult because of both a lack of commitment by executive staff and limited understanding of the methods and purposes of formal planning. Moreover, it was also found that companies had a constant need to call the planners back into the firm to overcome blockages and resolve problems which developed through the installation of the system. A general disillusionment set in which created a considerable market resistance to those professional service companies engaged in this field. The basis of this resistance was, however, largely overcome by one group of consultants. They extended their services beyond just developing and installing a suitable planning system for the company. They also offered to leave the company at the end of the project with a capability to resolve its own problems and to adjust and develop the original system as internal and external changes demanded it.

Similarly, Factors very quickly found that they could offer their customers not only the services of quick settlement of accounts, but a new 'package' in the form of the total handling of their sales ledger, thereby relieving the customer of many administration and accountancy problems.

Whatever the reasons for a new purchase, the role of the marketer is clear-cut—to communicate the existence and superiority of the substitute service. As with all new purchase situations, the provision of information is crucial. The extrinsic approach of extolling the virtues of the new service may provide a useful background, but a convincing demonstration of superiority of the service for the *potential buyers* will be needed even to obtain consideration of the service.

The way in which the replacement service is superior in the exact circumstances of the problem will require explanation, clarification, and demonstration. At the same time, the reasons for the loss of confidence in the existing service, or for its apparent anachronistic characteristics, must be understood if the substitute service is not to be subjected to similar criticism.

The loss of confidence in training by means of lectures with blackboard and easel does not imply confidence in a new training service that substitutes the tape cassette for the teacher and the slide projector for the blackboard. The 'plus' of such a change may well be that a totally portable system enables training to take place in less formal, less time-structured situations, and by programmed learning, while still preserving pupil participation.

Traditionally, cashflow problems were solved by overdrafts or short-term loans. The postwar emergence of Factoring services offered a new facility and a new method of overcoming liquidity problems. By using Factors, the supply firm could be sure of cash as soon as the goods were delivered without the need for lengthy negotiations and the provisions of guarantees and collateral which accompany a request to a commercial bank to make funds available. The advantage to the supplier is that the transaction is usually completed when the Factor has paid him, since it becomes the Factor's responsibility to collect the 'receivables' from the buyer of the goods.

Using the traditional commercial banking systems, even after the loan was granted, the risk of it being called in at, perhaps, a moment of acute embarrassment to the borrower was high and, in any event, it had to be repaid irrespective of the status of the debt which it was borrowed to cover. But the drawbacks of the Factoring system also need to be considered, most particularly its high cost relative to traditional sources of funds. The respective advantages and disadvantages vary in importance and weight in differing circumstances and to different firms. The marketer needs to understand this and to present his service accordingly.

Guidelines for the marketer
It has long been thought sufficient to describe empathy as one of the essential qualities of a salesman. Unfortunately, precisely what 'empathy' implies within the context of selling is difficult to explain. The elusive quality of 'empathy' might be said to include an awareness of the buying circumstances (straight repurchase, modified repurchase, new purchase) and the stage of the buying process which has been reached. The concepts of minimizing

uncertainty, understanding problems, and demonstrating professionalism take on a new and important realism when they are seen against the continuum of the buying process. The division of selling into extrinsic and intrinsic approaches is also highly practical if it, too, is related to the buying situation and process.

Any attempt to freeze the situation into a schematic representation is not likely to be successful as an action indicator, because there will be so many variables. However, setting out the situation has the inestimable advantage of showing the interaction of purchasing and marketing. Figure 7.1 which follows is no more than a snapshot of a new purchase situation. The incidence, direction, and strength of the marketing functions will vary in a modified repurchase and straight repurchase position. For example, the emphasis is removed from literature in a straight repurchase, although personal selling never ceases to be important.

All three buying situations call for varying degrees of information from maximum for a new purchase to minimal for a straight repurchase. The volume, the content, the timing, and the presentation of the information will depend upon the stage of the buying process reached. In the pre-sell period, information will tend to be general and extrinsic, while at the analysis of the offers stage it will be highly explicit and intrinsic. The important aspect is that the correct members of the decision-making unit obtain the information they need relevant to the area of their decisions at the moment at which they need it. The coordination of these variables is the key to the whole marketing process, whether it be for professional services or processed peas.

To focus the marketing effort and the information process, the checklist shown in Appendix B has been devised to provide some guidelines and to ensure that no major omissions occur in the marketing process or in communication.

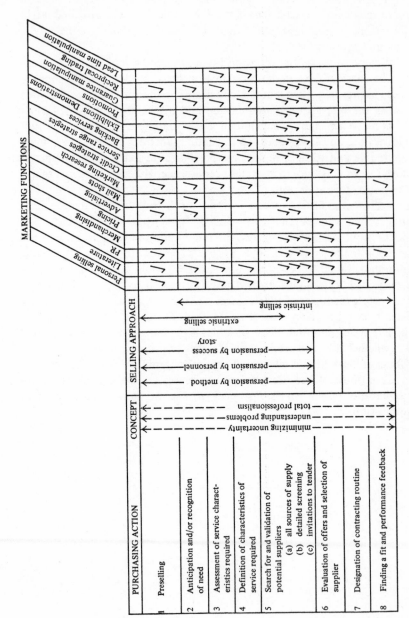

Figure 7.1. Purchasing and marketing interface

8

Identifying market opportunities

For some marketers, at least, early and correct identification of a market opportunity represents the major task, while for others the opportunities develop without any aid from the marketing company and the problem becomes one of closing the sale. Since marketing is concerned with seeking out opportunities as much as with satisfying them, the question of identifying where an opportunity exists or can be created is very much part of the total marketing process set out in chapter 2, 'Marketing and Selling'.

This identification of an opportunity is, of course, at its simplest the identification of a need for a service, whether or not the prospective user of the service recognizes the need. This, in turn, draws in the first of the marketing functions, marketing research. If the definitions offered of professional services and of consumer and producer services are accepted, then it becomes clear that the branch of marketing research required to probe professional services is industrial marketing research, not consumer research.

Traditionally, marketing research has been seen as a process by which facts concerning the sale and transfer of goods and services are gathered, recorded, analysed, and reported on. Ideas and data are collected from many sources and form the basis for action founded on logical analysis and judgement. Measurement is the foundation of science and classification is the basis of measurement. This dictum applies with equal force to marketing as to physics, but good marketing research does not simply comprise compilation, measurement, and classification. It is not just a study of secondary material in the hope that some usable data may be yielded, in the manner of the archaeologist turning over every stone in the hope that at least some will contribute to the understanding and interpretation of the past. Research properly conducted is an organized, highly methodical and planned procedure to increase knowledge and understanding of the subject under review, as a basis for informed decision-making.

Marketing men blessed with a strong intuitive approach may not require information, but for the less gifted majority of the business population, data on markets are vital for the successful creation of a marketing strategy that is meaningful both in terms of achievement and profitability. However, the view still exists that it is not possible to probe the demand for services in the same depth and with the same accuracy as for products. Experience shows the contrary. The techniques of industrial marketing research are adequately documented in several books.[1] For the purpose of identifying market opportunities, it is better to concentrate on the *use* of research rather than its methods.

Is research needed?
While a plea for more information can always be made, it is nevertheless necessary to test whether, in any given circumstances, research is indeed required in order to make decisions and to devise a course of action. If the cost to yield ratio is not satisfactory, then it is imperative to consider whether to do research at all.

In deciding if research is needed, the use of a checklist will define the position:

- Why is information needed?
- What information is needed?
- What resources will be required to obtain it?
- What will be accomplished by its acquisition?
- When can the results stemming from its acquisition be obtained?
- What conditions must be met?

The answers will give a positive indication as to whether research should be initiated.

There is little that industrial marketing research cannot achieve given unlimited appropriations and time, neither of which are ever, or are ever likely to be, available. The researcher has to work within the limitations set by the organization, the environmental conditions, and the present state of the art, but it is useful to categorize the areas of research objectives which should be considered, even if not actually researched. Knowledge of what is not known is at least as important as the knowledge itself.

A useful six point categorization has been devised to provide generic areas for investigation.[2] These are:

- *What is going on?* The function of keeping management informed so that it can exercise control. Sales estimates, market shares, and sales

[1] See Bibliography, page 183.
[2] Joseph W Newman, 'Put Research into Marketing Plan', *Harvard Business Review* (Cambridge, Mass., March/April 1962).

potential are examples. The figures reflect what is happening, but do not in themselves explain it.

- *How do you account for it?* This is the idea-getting or hypothesis-formulating function. It can involve any number of steps designed to reveal more about the nature of people, things, and relationships.
- *Is the explanation valid?* The function here is that of checking on the validity and importance of ideas and tentative explanations.
- *What, then, should be done?* This step involves the reasoning from the evidence obtained as to the nature of the situation being studied and prescribing the alternative courses of action which appear to be appropriate.
- *What results can be expected?* Tests can be instituted to predict the outcome of the suggested alternative courses of action.
- *How successful was the action?* The function here is that of evaluating how well the chosen course of action achieved its purpose. It may include examination of sales figures, or tests to measure advertisement exposure or changes in knowledge or attitudes.

Under all these headings, industrial marketing research has a substantial contribution to make. However, generic headings do not necessarily assist in making requirements precise. Asking: 'How do you account for it?' may not lead to specific questions such as: 'What contribution did the need for accountancy expertise make towards the decision to invite quotations from only a limited number of firms?' There are clearly a vast range of questions which could be asked under each of Newman's headings.

Precisely what marketing research can do for the service company will depend upon its ability to conceptualize a market situation, to conduct the survey, and to act on the results. Applications for research are more numerous than profitable, and care is therefore needed in selecting topics for research to be sure that they are actionable, rather than just interesting; profitable, rather than just useful.

Some typical research objectives which can be attained in relation to professional service markets, and which differ only in emphasis from research into products markets, are summarized in Figure 8.1.

This figure represents no more than a summation of some of the more typical marketing research objectives. The huge range which can be covered can be appreciated from the checklist in the Appendix of *The Assessment of Industrial Markets.*[1]

The intelligent and profitable use of research in identifying opportunities for the sale of professional services, as was pointed out in chapter 2, 'Marketing and Selling', will be less to monitor the course of the marketing campaign

[1] Aubrey Wilson, *The Assessment of Industrial Markets.* Hutchinson (London, 1968) Pp. 257–377. The checklist printed as an action matrix is available separately. Industrial Market Research (London, 1970).

Identification and measurement of the markets
- total markets
- significant segments of individual markets
- market coverage—new markets for existing services, new services for existing markets, new services for new markets

Analysis of the characteristics of the markets
- customer needs for services, function of services
- desirable service features
- customer practices in seeking services
- customers' attitudes and activities
- competitive conditions, share of market, marketing service costs, and related practices
- required commercial conditions
- market, facilities, and competitive trends

Projection of the markets (5 or 10 year period)
- basic growth or decline forces
- identification of 'top out' conditions
- trends or changes in customers, type of new competing services
- environmental changes—social, economic, technical, political
- projection of total market value

Critical factors for successful operations in individual markets
- nature of the service market (industry-merchandised, selected account development)
- range of services to be offered
- key functions necessary to operate service
- costs, systems, and related factors

Projection of available share of the market
- projection of market share based on market trend
- degree to which competitive strengths and weaknesses may affect position
- extent to which improved operations can contribute to higher market share
- development of market share for 5 and 10 year period

Market development programme
A statement of objectives of programme
- functional requirements to implement programme
- organization for implementation
- action programmes related to organization facilities, business development, advertising, and promotion, etc.

Figure 8.1. Research objectives

than to influence its outcome—a totally different philosophy from that which prevailed in the past on the rare occasions when research was undertaken by professional service companies.

Segmenting the market
It is one thing to identify a market opportunity, but quite another to pinpoint the actual organizations within it. To say that there is a market opportunity

to sell literary agency services to authors of business books is to describe a situation. This description makes no contribution to locating authors and would-be authors of business books to offer the service to them.

Thus, a move from the generic to the specific is now needed. How is the individual 'prospect' identified and located? A combination of two approaches is needed. First, to structure the particular 'plusses' of the firm and to relate them to segments of the market most likely and able to use them; and, second, to draw a profile of customer companies and then apply it as a template to the market to see where the prospective customers conforming most closely to the profile exist.

Identifying the unique selling proposition (USP)

The service company has the initial task of identifying for itself the aspects of the service, the unique combination of circumstances or possession of resources which makes it the most suitable for the clients it serves. However, it is not generally the existence of particular skills or resources which represents the USP of the service company, but a mix of varying proportions which will produce a unique combination.

The simplest situation may be one in which a company has no particular skills or resources other than capacity to meet a demand at a particular moment. A solicitor able to handle an urgent criminal case immediately offers a unique advantage to the accused over any solicitor who cannot attend court that day. In fact, capacity or lead-time is the most common advantage companies can offer in a given situation where all else tends to be equal. However, it is not a 'plus' which can be built on since its very existence tends to destroy it.

The usual situation will be more complex. The two examples given in Figures 8.2 and 8.3 illustrate how each additional 'plus' narrows down the competition, but it also illustrates how each additional 'plus' narrows down the potential market.

The advantages and dangers of this particular approach are obvious. Any system of opportunity identification by the relation of skills or resources to the market must be modular. That is, the skills and resources should be capable of being rearranged to open up a number of market possibilities, not just the single market at the end of a sequence.

The service company must be capable not only of identifying its own strengths and weaknesses objectively, but also of appreciating how they measure against the project need as perceived. The technique of S-O-F-T analysis (Strength-Opportunity-Fault-Threat) was developed for the purpose of corporate planning, but this self-analysis method can be used for USP identification.[1]

---

[1] E P Learned, C R Christensen, K R Andrews, and W D Guth, *Business Policy—Texts and Cases*. Irwin (Homewood, Ill., 1969). Pp.175–183, and *Planning a Diversification Strategy* Industrial Market Research (London, 1970). Pp. 10–12.

The skill needed is to be able to isolate those features of a service and a company—but most particularly the appropriate combination of them—which apply to a given situation and then to communicate and promote these to the prospect.

The whole purpose of USP identification is as a criterion for segmentation, the reduction of a total market into more homogeneous subsections. Such an approach is inherent in any professional service with claims to an area of specialization. The lawyer's practice with a known reputation for criminal work has segmented a total market for legal services to one relatively narrow

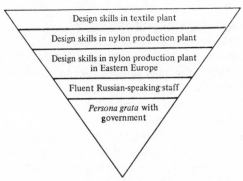

Figure 8.2. Unique selling proposition—textile plant

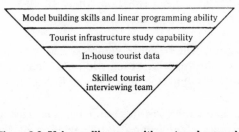

Figure 8.3. Unique selling proposition—travel research

section. The accountancy company, with special knowledge, experience, and staff familiar with taxation and business law and practice in tax-haven countries, has segmented a market on a geographical basis. These segmentations may be obvious, and they may be intentional, yet still not spring from a deliberate attempt to isolate the sector of the market most susceptible to the USP of the companies.

For most professional services, it is necessary to segment a market positively in order to concentrate resources on the segment offering the best potential opportunities compatible with the service company's corporate objectives and aspirations. Only when the segments are defined can the problem of identifying the prospect by name be attempted on a systematic basis.

Identifying the individual prospect

The service firm can start the individual identification process either from its own history of successes and failures in the area or, if it is a new area, from an examination of the characteristics of firms in the market segment.

The problem of identifying the individual firm will vary in complexity from service to service. In the case illustrated in Figure 8.2, the total number of organizations likely to want and to be capable of commissioning the building of nylon plant in Eastern Europe is limited to a small number of State organizations of Eastern European countries, and little effort is required to locate them.

Figure 8.3 illustrates a more complex situation. A much larger number of organizations may require the skills identified—State Tourist Boards, Government Economic Planning Departments, carriers, tour wholesalers, hotel developers and operators, construction companies, and a whole complex of other organizations and individuals who are concerned with tourism.

The total list of organizations can be coarse screened quickly to remove misfits and very low possibilities. Small organizations are unlikely to indulge in expensive model-building exercises. Underdeveloped countries seeking to improve tourist incomes invariably seek the aid of international organizations and governments of more advanced countries. Hotel operators' interests tend to be confined to the tourist market in which they operate, and they look towards tourist bodies and governments of the geographical areas involved to provide basic data. Small, feeder airline and private carriers' interests are usually circumscribed. Thus, the list can easily be narrowed down.

From here on, the service company can fine screen by using its own experiences or by examining the characteristics of the firms in the market segment. Based on the firm's experience it can identify the salient characteristics of:

- regular clients;
- sporadic clients;
- discontinued clients;
- non-clients (failed quotations);
- non-clients (no invitation to quote);
- others in the market.

Further questions requiring consideration are:

- What reasons underlie our being invited to quote against a particular inquiry?
- What reasons underlie our success on any particular contract?
- What reasons do we, and does the client, ascribe to our failure to obtain contracts? How far do the reasons accord?
- What are the reasons for sporadic rather than regular business?
- What is the history of each discontinued client account in the client category under consideration?

- What inquiries do we know have been made, but which we have not been invited to quote for, and what reasons do we and the prospective client ascribe to this situation?
- How many firms or organizations exist which use a similar service to that which we offer, but with which we have no contact?

An examination of the characteristics of clients for a service contract successfully obtained and fulfilled will provide an identification profile. But even without previous experience it is still possible to devise indicators of the existence of potential clients. Precisely which indicators are relevant is, of course, impossible to suggest without knowledge of the service and the specific market segments, but they will certainly be widespread and probably as many as 50 variables will be needed. Size, profitability, return on investment, possession of certain resources, organizational structure, location, employment of specialists within the company, extent of involvement with government, method of marketing, degree of verticalization, extent of cost-performance optimization, operations under cyclic demand, extent and efficiency of cost control, climate of labour relations, source of finance, and extent of forward planning: all have been found to have a significant effect alone or in combination on the susceptibility of a company to a marketing thrust by a service organization.

Identification of the relevant factors will enable the search to be concentrated on firms in the market corresponding as closely as possible to the profile drawn.

A series of experiments using this method was conducted by an American organization in 1969 and 1970 to identify potential clients for a long-range planning service. Like most organizations marketing services, they quickly realized that client interests tend to be very diverse and numerous, and that categorization was extremely difficult. Using an interactive graphic software package named PROMENADE, it proved possible to reduce the categorization problem to manageable proportions. Seventy-eight companies, whose membership status (long-range planning service or non-long-range planning service subscribers) was known, were used for 'training' the pattern recognition system. After 30 iterations through the data, the system became stable, forming two large groups of 'likely' and two smaller groups of 'unlikely' client companies. Then, an additional 59 companies were classified by the system. Of these, the long-range planning service membership of 30 was known. The system correctly classified 20 of these companies. Two of the companies selected by the system as being 'unlikely', but which were actually members when the data were collected several months earlier, had subsequently cancelled their membership. In addition, 4 unknown companies were selected as being likely prospects for membership of the long-range planning service.

The advantage of the PROMENADE method is illustrated in Figure 8.4

Without placing any quantities on the axes, the weighting of calls by average salesmen has been found to produce a preponderance of effort at the lower end of the scale of business possibilities. The above average salesman, with perhaps more empathy, a more intelligent approach to the sales job, and an entrepreneurial flair, shows a heavy call rate in the middle reaches of the possibilities of success. The PROMENADE method would seem to move both average and above average salesmen into the market sector where they can concentrate heavily on high 'prospects' for business.

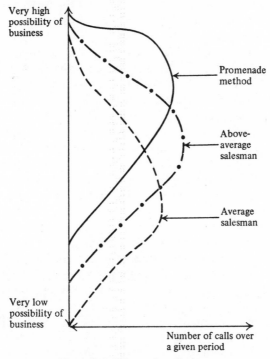

Figure 8.4. Salesman's call rate

The future possibilities of using this technique for marketing analysis in other areas are high, and its application could be useful. If prediction scores experienced so far are maintained, it will be a real breakthrough in application of cluster analysis in marketing.[1]

Clearly, few companies will have the resources to indulge in long computer-based experimental exercises, but the fundamental ideas underlying the prospect identification have clear implications for all professional service firms. The difficulties of correctly selecting the key criteria are no less than obtaining the criteria data both on client and non-client companies, but, even with inadequate data, much can be done along these lines.

[1] *Compact*, an internal journal of Stanford Research Institute (Menlo Park, Calif., February 1970).

Identifying a prospective purchasing company does not, of course, lead to the active decision-makers in the company. The decision-making unit, it has already been pointed out, varies from purchase to purchase, from time to time, and, most importantly, as a result of the situation which occasioned the purchase. Thus, it is quite impossible to designate in specific terms how a DMU may be composed at any particular moment. However, it is possible to build up a dossier over a period on DMU compositions by job title or definition under varying circumstances, so that a pattern emerges. This patterning may be by the activity or industry of the user of services, by size of company, by type or extent of service under consideration, or by using any of the criteria listed on page 77.

Some preliminary patterns can be obtained from *How British Industry Buys*[1] and, although much older, its Canadian and USA equivalents *How Industry Buys*[2] as well as from the Marketing Science Institute's work on industrial purchasing,[3] but the essential need is for each service company to develop information which enables a patterning to be obtained for the areas of business in which it has its major interests.

The information is extremely useful as a profile guide to the correct people to contact in a would-be purchasing company, and it is always relatively easy to identify the individual by name once the job title or function is known.

However, it is necessary to keep prospect identification in perspective, because it is unreal to examine it outside the context of the total and continuing market effort. It is part and parcel of a two-way communication process since informative and persuasive communications can materially assist in locating organizations which offer opportunities for business to the professional service company. Thus, identifying applications for a service and the individuals within the company with whom the decision-making authority lies is one part, albeit an early one, of the marketing activity, but it is one which will govern the strength, direction, and content of the whole marketing effort.

[1] *How British Industry Buys*. Institute of Marketing and Industrial Market Research Ltd. Hutchinson (London, 1967).

[2] D H Thain, *How Industry Buys*. School of Business Administration, University of Western Ontario (London, Canada, 1959). Also John H Platton, 'How Industry Buys' *Scientific American* (New York, 1955).

[3] P J Robinson et al., *Industrial Buying and Creative Marketing*. Allyn & Bacon (Boston, Mass., 1967). Pp. 83–85.

9

Market strategy and planning

It has already been emphasized that to discuss the creation of marketing strategies and planning systems divorced from the context of the firm's corporate planning is to create an unreal, indeed a dangerous, situation. Corporate strategy has been defined as 'the pattern of objectives, purposes or goals and major policies and plans for achieving these goals, stated in such a way as to define what business the company is in or is to be in and the kind of company it is or is to be.' Thus, strategic marketing decisions and their methods of implementation are only a subsection of the firm's total planning activity, and they must be compatible with that activity. It is important that they are seen this way.

There are several fundamental steps which precede the formulation and adoption of marketing strategy. At their simplest, they would involve:

- monitoring the current position;
- identifying those activities of the firm where the emphasis must be changed by reduction, expansion, or redirection;
- auditing the firm's strengths, resources, and weaknesses;
- corporate objective setting.

These activities, which may not necessarily be undertaken in the order given, have to be carried out if the realistic and realizable objectives for the firm are to be defined accurately. The processes described will reveal any quantitative and qualitative resource gaps which must be filled to achieve the targets. The existence of any gaps and other factors will lead to a recycling of the planning steps including revision of objectives until the hoped-for optimum matching of opportunities and resources indicate them to be practical, and also the timespan required for their achievement. It is from this point that the marketing strategies can be developed, and while they are considered in isolation in this chapter their interconnection with, and relevance to, the corporate strategies and plans must be constantly kept in view.

The contention throughout this book has been that the marketing of intangibles usually requires different approaches and methods from those involved in the marketing of products. Two mutually exclusive schools of thought exist as to the applicability of product-marketing techniques. The first is that they are totally inapplicable to the marketing of intangibles. The second view takes the opposite posture, maintaining that there is no fundamental difference between the marketing techniques required to move goods or services towards the final consumer.[1] The answer, as in most situations where the position is described in extremes, is somewhere down the middle: that is with suitable adaptations some product-marketing techniques are applicable under different circumstances. Figure 2.1, page 23, shows that the differences between products and services marketing are greater than can be dismissed as incidental, but the extent of the similarities is substantial. The suggestion that product-marketing techniques are either totally suitable or totally unsuitable is, in fact, untenable.

Background—ethical considerations

The attitude of what has been termed the 'consultant professions'—for example, those of law, medicine, architecture, accountancy—towards marketing has been largely attributed to the ethical considerations involved in its practice. It has been held that the essence of the professional approach to obtaining business is that it should be allowed to come without being actively sought by the practitioners. Whether such an attitude is 'anti-marketing' or just 'no marketing' is of no consequence because either way it represents a total rejection of any obvious attempt to seek out business. The 'no-marketing' case has been made out elegantly and in great detail by F.A.R. Bennion who, it might be said, represents the attitudes typical in the senior profession to any suggestion of 'trade'. The disdain and distaste for all forms of promotion which Bennion expresses and seeks to justify comes out clearly in a Freudian titled chapter, 'Touting and Canvassing'.[2]

Active advertising and sales promotion are too often regarded as placing the professional service in an unprofessional atmosphere. Precisely what is unethical about marketing or the activities which constitute the sum total of marketing has never been adequately expressed in terms which are valid. The Law Society's view that prohibition of advertising is necessary to preserve the dignity of the profession, at the kindest, can only be described as doctrine for more leisurely times. If it is true, then by implication engineering con-

---

[1] See Wittreich, 'How to Buy/Sell Professional Services', *Harvard Business Review* (Cambridge, Mass., March/April 1961). Also Everett Turner, 'Marketing Professional Services', *Journal of Marketing* (Chicago, October 1969).

[2] F. A. R. Bennion, *Professional Ethics*. Charles Knight (London, 1969). Chapter 11

sultancy, banking, financial services, and contract R & D are undignified. The Bar Council, with monumental lack of understanding of marketing and of business, stated that: 'If barristers were to advertise, the advantages would go, not to the best qualified, but to the barristers with the longest purse and the least scruples.'[1] Once again, it might be asked, if this were true, how in other disciplines do small professional firms which do not advertise succeed in existing alongside large ones who do, and are the professional firms who advertise less qualified than the firms who do not, and do they have less scruples?

The Secretary of State for Industry and Trade requested the professions examined in the Monopolies Commission Report to re-examine their restrictive practices in the light of the guidance given in that report. A summary of replies from the Royal Institution of Chartered Surveyors, the Law Society, the Royal Institute of British Architects, and the British Medical Association, to take only four groups, indicates a virtually complete rejection of the Monopolies Commission recommendations and, indeed, a counter-attack in the form that the Commission was 'a body entirely inappropriate for the study of the professions'.[2]

To market or not to market is a decision for the individual company and for the professional bodies which are in a position to control the behaviour of their members. Perhaps because of the high esteem in which the senior professions are held, and because of the urgent personal need of many individuals in what might be termed the less accepted or less prestigious professions to obtain acceptance, there has been a strong tendency to follow old-established professional practices. Thus, the 'no marketing' attitude has permeated into most groups and activities which would like to be regarded as professions in the same manner as are the 'closed professions'.

The Monopolies Commission report on professional services called for a review of practices, and found collective price fixing and restrictions on advertising, to take only two marketing activities, as likely to be against the public interest.[3] That it should have concluded this is understandable because there is nothing unethical about selling or advertising which is designed to promote a professional service or to inform potential users about that service. The danger comes not from the advertising or price competition as such, but from the danger common in all transactions: false and exaggerated claims, badly designed or made goods (or their service equivalent—incompetently rendered service).

Indeed, the confusion in the professions concerning the ethical limits of advertising is typified by the fact that, while in some professions there is a

---

[1] Bar Council submission to the Monopolies Commission, quoted by F. A. R. Bennion, op. cit. P. 154.

[2] *RICS News.* (London, 12 May 1971).

[3] Monopolies Commission, *Professional Services.* HMSO (London, 1970). Paras. 320 and 347.

ban on advertising by individuals, the professional associations use established promotional techniques, as in the case of the Law Society.

The dialectics are fascinating, but do not advance the discussion on the application of marketing to professional services. If the societies which control or represent professional service companies and practitioners choose to limit or bar marketing, there may be tenable reasons, and the fact that they often have mandatory powers over their members to practise their profession means that there is little the individual can do except to seek to change the whole system. Where membership of a professional association is not a condition of practice, and restraints on marketing cannot be made to apply to non-association members, then the results of this self-imposed handicap on association members must be laid firmly at the door of the professional body.

How then can professional service firms not bound, or not choosing to be bound, by restrictive and outdated practices, market their services in a positive and acceptable way? Consideration of the concepts and methods available to them must commence with the study of strategic factors.

Strategies and tactics: A differentiation

Considerable confusion exists in marketing between strategy and tactics, but it is a confusion that occurs in almost all business activities. Military definitions (strategies are the deployment of forces in a war situation to defeat an enemy in pursuit of goals prescribed by leaders of state) and political definitions (the application of national resources to accomplish national goals) provide a starting point for distinguishing strategic and tactical plans and actions. In a business, strategy might be defined as the creation and implementation of plans, devised to accomplish long-term objectives and, as such, they are likely to induce major changes in the relationship between the firm and its competitive environment. Tactics are concerned with activities directed to achieve short-term objectives.

However, 'short' and 'long' terms are relative to total timespans, and can be interpreted in many ways. Thus, for many activities, if defined on a time continuum, it becomes arguable as to whether they are, in fact, strategic or tactical.

The individual marketing functions, with the exception of new 'product' development, tend to be applied tactically rather than strategically, since they are usually directed to achieve short-term aims; the pricing objectives may be to obtain a firmer foothold in a particular market segment; the advertising campaign to develop sales of a specific part of the service mix; and the PR campaign to obtain credibility in a particular activity. Even if all three were directed to achieving sales in the long term, they remain tactical in that 'long-term sales' may, in turn, be directed to achieve the strategic objectives of, say, a given return on investment.

The concept of marketing strategy differs somewhat in the way it is practised from the way it is propounded in marketing literature. In marketing planning, however, strategy tends to break down into two or three generally accepted groups: (a) segmentation, the selection of market targets; (b) marketing mix, the combination of the various marketing functions; and (c) product or service mix. Service mix, it can be argued, is a separate strategy, but its impact on the marketing strategy is so pervasive that a strong case can be made out for its inclusion as one component of the marketing strategy. The advantage of treating it as part of the overall marketing strategy and not as a separate substrategy is that it ensures compatibility with the total plan.

The most difficult of questions to resolve is inherent in the very blurred lines between strategic and tactical decisions; that is, should the long-term strategies be adhered to or should adjustment be made in the light of the reality revealed by the short-term tactical operations? There can be strong arguments for resolutely pursuing the stated objectives through the selected strategies and for rational adjustment to reach *attainable* targets. While it is absurd not to make adjustments in the light of changes which have occurred, it is equally foolish to abandon long-term strategic targets and policies in response to each variation from the anticipated results or the agreed approaches. Because tactics are essentially short term and flexible, it is these that should be modified to ensure the master strategy can be maintained so long as the objectives remain realizable. The adjustment in tactics will inevitably alter the marketing mix which must always be most sensitive and responsive to change.

Setting strategic objectives

Objectives, the core of managerial action, provide direction to the marketing team by defining targets, the path to their attainment, and the action necessary to achieve them. Objectives can be expressed in many ways, but basically they group into time dimensions or scope dimensions, or relate to a designated area within the firm. Objectives can be expressed for any functional area or organizational level considered important as well as for the firm itself.

The first step in developing suitable strategies is the acceptance by all concerned of the objectives of the company and of the route to be followed to achieve these over a given time scale. Without this prior agreement, there is little likelihood of any marketing strategy being successful or of objectives being achieved in a structured rather than a reactive manner.

The setting of marketing objectives is best accomplished in four stages, but the importance of a disciplined approach to objective setting and of devising a system which will achieve them, cannot be overstated. Although concerned primarily with corporate planning, but applicable and adaptable to marketing, Igor Ansoff's approach to objective setting is relevant and practical, and is well worth close study and adoption.[1]

The first stage is to decide precisely what business the professional service firm is in. The merchant banks, which have grown over two centuries from

[1] Igor Ansoff, *Corporate Strategy*. McGraw-Hill (New York, 1965). Chapter 3.

themselves being merchants, may now see their role as providing commodity confirming services, short-term finance, or public floatation, which are relatively narrow activities, or they may offer aids for achieving higher financial productivity which covers a very much wider spectrum. The conceptualization of the content and application of the services offered is fundamental to objective setting. Reference to page 18 will show that a generic definition of the services offered is a necessary precondition to establishing objectives and targets as well as for market planning.

At the second stage, the broad company objectives must be related to key-result areas, that is those in which success is vital to the firm, and which can be measured, preferably against quantified objectives. Market penetration and the growth rate of sales are examples of key-result areas.

The third stage is the setting of sub-objectives to accomplish the broad company objective—for example, higher sales volume, wider customer base, geographical expansion.

The fourth and final step is the use of the designated key-result areas to serve as yardsticks for the sub-objectives.

The last two steps are recycled until specific objectives have been created for the marketing team down to its lower levels. At each succeeding level of management, sub-objectives are checked for inconsistencies and conflicts, horizontally with sub-objectives of other departments, and vertically with the broader company objectives.

Devising a marketing strategy

Clearly, it is not possible to define specific strategies which can be taken either wholly or piecemeal and applied to any particular service or circumstance. What is required is an understanding of precisely what comprises marketing strategies and their different types. A grasp of these essentials enables a marketing strategy to be developed and implemented. Then, within its framework, it is possible to define appropriate tactical inputs and apply the correct combination of marketing tools.

Given that a service firm has made its generic service definition, has decided what market it is in, and has clearly identified its objectives, it is now necessary for it to consider the three components of the marketing strategy —market segmentation, marketing mix, and service mix.

Market segmentation serves two very basic purposes: first, to differentiate the service and the service firm from all others, thus creating a special and selective demand for the service differentiated, and, second, to offer what is a direct appeal to particular segments of the total market which at present purchase services according less closely to their requirements than the differentiated service. The criteria for segmentation will vary from firm to firm, but the starting point must be the identification of the firm's strengths and resources, since a segmentation strategy not based on strength cannot succeed. The other major consideration is need identification. At some point, the two must meet if segmentation is to work. It may be necessary to build strengths and resources to fill the need or to seek to educate or persuade the buyers of professional services to modify their needs to make the services offered acceptable.

While it is perfectly possible for a service company to prosper within a single and narrow segment, for most companies there will be a number of segments with differing degrees of attractiveness. These must be ordered in priority so that the resources of the company can be concentrated on the top-priority groups, moving to lower priorities only when penetration of those more highly rated has been achieved.

The advantages of intelligently applied segmentation policies are that they enable a firm to focus firmly on its target customer groups and to direct its marketing activities to the group. The benefit to the service company is practical and in image terms is considerable.

The second major component of marketing strategy is the marketing mix, that is the decisions concerning the types, strength, and weight of the various marketing activities which will be used to achieve the targets. The choice for those firms marketing professional services is almost as wide as that for companies marketing products. While the obvious activities, such as personal selling, press and direct mail advertising, and PR, come to mind at once, within professional service companies there has been an almost total neglect of merchandising and pricing.

The strategic decisions to be made concern which techniques will be used, when they will be used, and how they will be used. The decisions are, of course, influenced by the segmentation priorities and the service mix, but at the same time the choice and availability of techniques will also influence the segmentation and service-mix policy.

The third component of the marketing strategy (although, as has been pointed out, it is arguable whether it should be included) is the service mix; that is, precisely what range of services should be offered within the market. While it was unthinkable 20 years ago that an accountancy firm would provide anything other than accountancy services, the development of a management consultancy capability by a number of accountancy companies is now accepted as a logical, if controversial, addition to their service mix. Similar developments in banking and architectural services can also be easily identified. The introduction of a range of services as opposed to a single service, whether through opportunistic growth or as a deliberate and planned policy, is always an important strategic decision. Once again, the interdependability of the elements within the marketing strategy is obvious, since the segmentation and marketing-mix policies adopted must influence the service mix choice; the converse is also true.

Factors impacting on strategy
The marketing strategy and activities will be taking place within a highly

dynamic environment; thus the tactical policies which contribute to the total strategy cannot be ignored. The interweaving of shorter-term policies within the fabric of the total marketing strategy calls for extreme skill, care, sensitivity to the strengths and weaknesses of the firm, the threats and opportunities present within the environment, and a flow of recent, accurate, and detailed information. Precisely which strategy or combination of strategies will be adopted depends upon the specific circumstances of the service company and its resources, as well as the corporate and marketing objectives.

In order to decide which marketing activities are appropriate to the strategies adopted, a further group of seven factors besides those of segmentation, marketing, and service mix require consideration. These are:

1 Customer variables: The number of buyers in the market; their purchases, motives, needs, attitudes, and purchasing habits.
2 Environmental variables: Economic activity, social trends, and government activities.
3 Competitive variables: Policies of other companies offering similar and substitute services.
4 Marketing decision variables: Any factor under the control of the firm which may be used to stimulate the firm's sales. These could include the mix of services offered and the communication mix.
5 Marketing allocation variables: Division of the firm's marketing efforts among its services, customers, segments, and sales areas.
6 Market response variables: Behaviour of sales in response to alternative levels, allocations, and mixes of marketing effort.
7 Resource variables: Availability of resources—personnel, finance, equipment, and facilities.

The interrelationship between the variables and the major strategies is complex and is constantly changing. They might perhaps best be likened to a solar system with the major strategies forming a sun which carries with it seven planets represented by the variables. These variables, like planets, move in highly eccentric ellipses, and their relationship with the sun is far from constant. The analogy can go no further, however, since unlike the solar system the paths of the various bodies cannot be predicted with accuracy. The position might, however, be illustrated as shown in Figure 9.1.

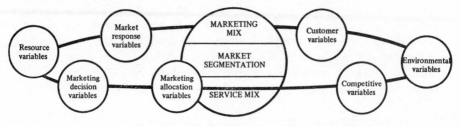

Figure 9.1.

Selection of the strategy and consideration of its elements leads back to the steps which must be taken to implement the strategy. These were set out in detail in chapter 2, 'Marketing and Selling', but are restated here within the context of strategic planning.

1 Generic service definition.
2 Target group definition.
3 Differentiated marketing decisions.
4 Customer behaviour analysis.
5 Identification of differentiated advantages.
6 Communication mix determination.
7 Integration of marketing activities.
8 Introduction of routines for continuous market feedback.
9 Auditing of the marketing effort and results.

The adoption of a marketing strategy requires the coordination of all the marketing activities with a common objective—the needs and wants of the customer. Nevertheless, the direction of a company's activities to the satisfaction of these needs must be compatible with its resources and objectives, and it is this restraint which significantly alters the marketing approach of firms offering similar services in identical markets.

Market planning

To accomplish the task of client satisfaction, it is necessary to develop interrelated strategies directed towards this goal. A market strategy cannot be implemented effectively unless it forms part of a total plan which has been budgeted and scheduled. If there is to be formal, consistent, and purposeful marketing, planning is a vital activity. The purpose of market planning is to ensure that objectives are achieved through the selected strategy and its component tactical inputs, that the total marketing effort is directed towards these ends, and is compatible with the overall corporate plan.

It is suggested by H R Dodge that there are four preconditions for success in planning the market development of a company.[1] These are:

- a total commitment to the marketing concept of a customer-creating, customer-satisfying organism;
- coordinated structuring of the marketing functions;
- coordination of action within the agreed programme;
- gradualism in the integration process.

Given that these are accomplished, the effectiveness of the strategic planning and operations may nevertheless be partially lost because of the confusion between tactics and strategies and because management spends most of its time on operational or tactical planning to the detriment of the longer-term issues involved in strategic decisions and objectives.

[1] H R Dodge, *Industrial Marketing*. McGraw-Hill (New York, 1970). P. 50.

The role of organizations in planning
Organizations have three major purposes:

- to divide tasks in an orderly fashion so as to provide for their effective performance—specialization;
- to ensure consistency and to develop correct timing for tasks—co-ordination;
- to assign authority and responsibility.

It is perhaps the second task, coordination, which is the most difficult to achieve within the context of marketing. The customer sees the firm's marketing only as the manifestation of the sum total of all the activities involved and not as separate activities which he evaluates individually. Thus, the different marketing activities must support each other and be performed in the correct sequence at the correct place. But the optimum mix of form, time, place, and possession will only remain so for a relatively short while, since the common characteristic of most markets is change. The objectives of the coordination activities must themselves alter in response to change. Part of the function of coordination is to identify change, the alternatives that change opens up in terms of marketing mix and tactics and the design and implementation of the marketing operations in response to these factors.

While coordination is easy to postulate, achieving it is extremely difficult. The *sine qua non* for effective coordination is good communications, whatever the channels for these may be. Communication, together with understanding and acceptance of mutually agreed overall objectives, does not guarantee co-ordination, but does at least make it possible.

The need for an efficient information system is obvious, whether it is for total management information systems or systems related strictly to the marketing activities. Management information systems, despite their currently stylish overtones and, thus, the danger of abandonment as the fashions in management philosophies and techniques change, have an important contribution to make towards the efficiency and profitability of the market effort. Management information systems encourage systematic planning and an intelligent, scientific approach to determining an organization's information needs and in developing and operating a system which is conducive to sound decision-making.

Because most professional service companies are small, it is improbable that they will install advanced computer-based management information systems, and, indeed, it may be impractical for them to do so. However, there is a great deal to be learned from such systems which enable small-scale manual versions to be developed and operated. The plea is for systemization of information gathering and dissemination, rather than leaving it to the vagaries of the marketing process or the personnel involved.

A good marketing organization is one which is flexible, has great potential, and in which there is a common acceptance of a central philosophy or tradition. This, too, is easy to postulate, but difficult to achieve. Without flexibility it cannot cope with change; without an ability to grow profitably it can at best only survive, and without a central philosophy or tradition it cannot coordinate.

The marketing organization can be founded on a number of different bases, the most common being geographic, service range, customer, or function. Because of the limited size and resources of most professional service firms geographic divisions are relatively rare, although they are not unknown. Multinational and national service organizations do exist in, for example, insurance, banking, architecture, and advertising. Moreover, the geographical organization enables the mix to be adjusted more narrowly to the needs of the area than is possible with broader territorial coverage. Thus, the appeals have a particular relevance and the analogies used in, for example, the 'selling by success story' can be particularly apposite.

Organization by type of service is much more commonplace in professional services. In banking, for example, it might be represented by trustee services, loans, commercial intelligence; in an architectural firm by town planning, mechanical and electrical services, and economic viability studies.

Organizations based upon customer type are found mainly, but not exclusively, in the larger professional service firms. Examples can be found of contract R & D organizations divisionalized on the basis of serving mechanical engineering, industrial and consumer electronics, life sciences, and forest products. Organization on a 'trade' basis has the advantage of enabling the marketing to be sharply focused on customers' needs and problems, and of being able to build up super-specialization and credibility. It also enables the client contact to develop in a highly personal way, since generally only one salesman is required to look after the needs of customers in each segment. It has the disadvantage of limiting cross-fertilization on interdisciplinary or other bases.

Organization based on marketing functions is a logical outcome of specialization. It offers the benefit of highly trained specialists in each function, for example, personal selling, advertising, PR, and marketing research, and can be centred around whichever specific functions or activities are assigned and organized.

The four approaches are not mutually exclusive and a combination of several of them may yield the optimum organizational structure. One grouping might be by type of customer, by type of service, and by geographical area. Thus, a property management firm could divide its marketing efforts between the industrial, commercial, agricultural, and domestic sectors with specialist personnel able to provide management, development, and investment services. These specialists would be available on a regional basis.

The test of a good marketing organization is whether tight, quickly applied but insightful control is exercised through accurate function definition and realistic objectives; whether coordination is systematic and structured to encourage cooperation; whether information flows quickly, accurately, and regularly in both directions along communication channels; and whether the whole structure can respond without distortion or fracture to environmental or internal changes.

Market measurement and control

A number of adjectives have been used to describe the desirable features of organizations: 'effective', 'efficient', 'good', 'creative'. These are relative terms and can only apply if they relate to some measurement of total performance as a whole as well as of the performance of components, such as marketing. Clearly, performance must be seen as comparative, that is: comparison with the stated objectives and how far they have been achieved; comparison with the methods devised to achieve the objectives and how these methods have been realized; comparison with competitive performance; and, finally, comparison with the performance of the market as a whole. It is not without significance that measurement (or monitoring) and control are almost invariably grouped together in books on marketing. They are insolubly linked because control cannot be effective without standards of performance.

Aside from the achievement of objectives there are other criteria for developing and for evaluating standards of performance. They group conveniently under the headings:

- profit;
- costs;
- market share;
- sales.

While in large concerns the marketing department can often be treated as accountable for profit or loss in its own right, it would be rare to find such an arrangement in the professional service firm. Nevertheless, the contribution of marketing to total profitability requires assessment, if only because of the essentially variable nature of marketing costs. The ability of a firm to measure profitability in its marketing operations as distinct from the total profitability of the firm will vary with the firm's size, the complexity of its operations, and the range of services offered. For small firms, there is ample evidence to show that the administrative and accounting methods it is necessary to install to measure and control performance are often out of all proportion to the results achieved. Thus, for professional services firms (and not ignoring the need for at least an outline idea of profit contribution), measurement and control is better achieved through cost control.

Cost control is a necessary operating objective of a firm. One way in which a firm tries to achieve its profit objectives is to administer its expenditure to get the maximum results from the costs it incurs. Thus, marketing activities, which stem from the marketing strategy, must be subject to cost accounting procedure to enable management to make periodic comparisons of marketing costs in terms of the specific origins of these costs. The statement can be used both as a standard of performance and as an instrument of cost control.[1] A comparison of costs over a period of time, and also with averages for the profession as a whole (where these are available), is one of the more conventional ways to approach the measurement and control of performance.

A frequently used standard of measurement of the success of marketing strategy and overall marketing effectiveness is market share; the use of this criterion is not without its critics. A decline in a total market may leave a company with a smaller sales volume, but the same or even increased percentage of total business. Another objection is that market share analysis ignores the profit element of the operation. The fact that market share analyses do not incorporate profit studies means that they cannot be combined with profit/cost analyses in attempts to achieve some correlation. The advantages of market share studies as a measure of performance, aside from the fact that they are relatively simple and easy to understand and provide a common basis for comparing one firm with another, are that in appraising performance they largely avoid the problem of accountability for forces in the market over which the service firm has no control, and thus relate largely to the firm's performance and effectiveness.

Whatever the advantages may be, market size and trend information for professional service markets is rarely available on a regular basis and usually has to be obtained by one-off research projects which makes market share analyses a costly procedure.

Perhaps the simplest measure of a strategy's effectiveness and of performance is sales volume, but this is not a measure that can be used in isolation, since it must be related to market share position to be meaningful and, more importantly, suffering as it does, like market share analysis, from lack of profit gearing, it can be misleading. The costs of achieving any given sales volume will be the determinant of whether a company should be in the market at all.

As is common in marketing, it is probably a combination of factors rather than a single aspect which will provide for the individual firm the optimum method for assessing the effectiveness of its marketing activities. However, there will have to be considerably more information on the size, structure, and trends of markets for individual services before measurement of performance will reach even the fairly crude standards achieved by the goods producing industries.

There is, however, little point in setting up complex monitoring and detailed measuring systems if there is no intention of attempting to control the phenomenon reported. Thus, a vital part of the process of setting up measurement systems is to develop an equivalent control system.

Control of marketing programmes which results from the implementation

[1] J B Matthews et al., Marketing—An Introductory Analysis. McGraw-Hill (New York, 1964). Pp. 506–514.

of the strategy, like control of any other management activity, should be a dynamic process responding to changes as they occur. In short, it is the continuous process by which management makes certain that the strategies are adopted, are implemented, guided, or restrained to achieve the goals which they have been devised to attain. It cannot be effective if practised in a one-off or reactive way.

It is obvious that effective control cannot be achieved unless information is available—something which has been stressed throughout this book. The flow of information from the centre on plans and programmes must be communicated to all departments and individuals involved to ensure co-ordination of effort. Of equal importance, critical information must flow back from the market to the centre to enable managers to decide if the marketing programme is following its planned course in terms of time and achievement.

Comparison of performance—the firm's and the market's—provides the trigger for applying the type of controls most suited to the situation; for example, costs moving out of line with budgets may call for cutbacks, switches, or total re-examination of the hypotheses on which the budgets were originally made; target accomplishment in sales volume with a reduction in profits may demand a shift in emphasis to the promotion of other services in the company's range or to other types of customers.

Constant monitoring and appraisal of the marketing strategy and marketing performance—sales, advertising, PR, and other elements in the marketing mix—will indicate the moment and the need for the imposition of controls. More advertising, less advertising, different advertising, can all be decided if there is some measure of advertising's contribution to the marketing effort.

The hazard to be avoided is the development of too complex methods of measurement and their appropriate controls in relation to the value which will be obtained from them in their implementation. The major difference between measurement and control in the marketing of professional services and in the marketing of products is largely one of scale. Because professional service firms tend to be small, total communication and awareness is usually high, so that subjective assessment is often easy if only because involvement of the professional tends to be more complete than is typical in marketing. The professional who can sell has an extensive knowledge of the service rendered and usually of the client problems, whereas the marketing man in a goods-producing industry usually tends to be a marketing specialist rather than a technician.

This advantage can, of course, be a danger in that professional firms tend to ignore simple methods of measurement and the application of formal controls. However, for the sentient, marketing-oriented firm, the disadvantages of size in terms of ability to develop specializations can be more than offset by the speed of communication, flexibility of operations, and the total interface it can achieve between company and customer.

Planning, of course, is only one activity involved in running a successful business, but it is a key element. The plan itself and the process of planning gives direction, cohesion, and thrust to the enterprise; they provide an improved focus on objectives and targets and, perhaps of equal importance, they stimulate heightened motivation to accomplishment.

10

Marketing functions: Personal selling

The implications of the buying situation require interpretation in terms of the individual marketing functions. In the final analysis, the marketer of services will need to know just how the various tools of marketing fit into the overall strategy, and how compatible they are with the three underlying concepts of professional service marketing.

There has already been reference in chapter 2 to the low status of marketing among many professional men and women, and their disdain and distaste for both the tools of marketing and the market place. The semantic road block which Wittreich so ably defines and describes[1] has prevented many professionals who can sell from doing so, and, clearly, selling and all the other methods of marketing will not be conducted effectively so long as the professional feels that marketing is incompatible with his professionalism.

However, once an acceptance of the marketing concept is achieved and a decision is made that the professional firm *will* market its services, then a further series of decisions must follow in relation to the marketing mix to be adopted. In consideration of precisely which activities will or will not be included, personal selling will tend to dominate.

Deciding to include personal selling in the marketing mix
The conditions under which personal selling rather than other elements in the marketing mix will become paramount are:

- when the market is concentrated or limited in some way;
- when the 'product' must be fitted to individual needs;

[1] Warren J Wittreich, *Selling—A Prerequisite to Success as a Professional*. (A paper presented at a conference in Detroit, Mich., 8 January 1969.)

- when the personality of the salesman is needed to establish *rapport* and build confidence.

It can be seen that these three conditions apply over a wide range of professional services such as insurance, management consultancy, engineering and design consultancy, loss adjusting, advertising, and PR. Not surprisingly, therefore, professional service firms which do market their services tend to lean heavily on the personal confrontation.

The characteristics of personal selling which distinguish it from other types of marketing activity can be seen to fit precisely the circumstances under which most professional services are offered to prospective buyers since it provides:

- flexibility—the message can be tailored precisely to the client's or prospect's needs;
- comprehensiveness—the most complex sales messages can be communicated and explained;
- attention-getting—under most circumstances personal selling obtains and maintains attention at a far higher level than other marketing techniques.

However, there is a negative attribute that cannot be ignored. Personal selling is costly, being labour intensive and of generally the most expensive kind. But for this restraint there might perhaps be no decision to make, since all selling could be undertaken in face to face encounters. The question is one entirely of cost effectiveness. Given a mix of market characteristics which lend themselves to the particular attributes of personal selling, the decision to include personal selling in the marketing mix becomes a relatively easy one to make. More difficult to decide is *who* sells, *how* do they sell, and *when* do they sell?

Who sells?
Apart from the salesman, most members of a firm who have any client contact sell or contribute to selling: from the professionals and their assistants actually on the job, to the receptionists and telephone operators in the office. The salesman's efforts will be supported or diluted by the image projected by others. A marketing oriented operation is one which is geared to presenting the firm and its services in the most favourable light at all times, but it is with personal selling that the interface between the buyer and seller will occur most frequently, and usually as the first part of the sales sequence. Thus, the responsibility on the salesman is considerable, and calls for a high degree of empathy and understanding. However, to suggest in professional service selling that personal selling is or should be confined to those allotted the role of selling would be to circumscribe unnecessarily the personal selling activity.

Clearly, besides the salesman the professional implementers of the services are themselves highly potent positive and negative sales influence, and to allow these personnel contact with clients and potential clients when they are not instructed in at least the rudiments of selling may well be disastrous for the selling effort, and may be dangerous in the extreme. For professional service firms more so than for those offering other intangibles or products, there will always exist a core of 'backroom boys', 'academics', 'practitioners', for whom nothing other than the elegant solutions of problems and application of sophisticated techniques will count. Their job satisfaction is in the efficient completion of the work in hand, irrespective of clients' changing needs, attitudes, perceptions, and on-going developments. These are the professionals who will never, by inclination and by personality, make professional salesmen or any type of salesmen, and it is useless to try to train or persuade them to be other than they are. What must be done, however, is to eliminate the negative aspect of their approach and to communicate the overriding requirement for 'satisfaction engineering', since the firm depends upon a flow of old and new clients to continue to exist. There is an old salesman's dogma that 'no one ever won an argument with a customer', and it is as good for professional services as for salesmen of potted shrimps.

Thus, a major task in developing personal selling approaches is to ensure that the base is not eroded by bad client relations at levels other than that of the salesman. The whole organization must be geared to the fact and MUST BELIEVE that the client comes first. If the salesman is not perpetually looking over his shoulder to ensure that his position is not being undermined by others, he can concentrate on the job in hand with confidence not only in what he is doing, but in what the professionals and the support staff are doing on the assignments he has obtained for them.

It has already been clearly indicated that the professional who can sell is the ideal person for selling professional services. Irrespective of his qualifications or abilities in his professional field, if he is a salesman, he will possess certain important characteristics which he will graft on to his technical expertise. 'Of course all selling requires certain basic qualities, although these qualities may be required with varying amounts of emphasis. Drive, determination to go on trying, personality, being a good listener, being conscious of one's prospect's reactions, have a "feel" of the sales situation.'[1]

The empathy and ego drive syndrome of the good salesman which has been described and explored many times, but nowhere better than by Mayer and Greenberg,[2] and its importance in industrial selling, cannot be overemphasized. However, it is the explorative capabilities which will distinguish the best sellers of professional services from the average. It is this which will induce a salesman to treat and examine each inquiry or prospect as an indi-

[1] David Rowe, 'Industrial Selling', *The Marketing of Industrial Products.* Aubrey Wilson, ed. Pan Books (London, 1972).
[2] D Mayer and H Greenberg, 'What Makes a Good Salesman', *Harvard Business Review* (Cambridge, Mass., July/August 1964).

vidual situation, unlike marketing research which adopts the macro-approach and reports on markets as a whole. Without this explorative interest the salesman will fail to fit his service to the buyer's needs, he will fail to locate the decision-making unit, and his lack of real interest in the customer will show through as disdain for the whole selling process.

In selling professional services, the salesman must take on a managerial as well as a communication and persuasive role. Because services cannot be sold without deploying the whole array of the professional firm's resources, the salesman must be capable of demonstrating the appropriate resources of the firm and ensuring that promises of quality, delivery, and services are kept. He must be capable of taking the initiative and of organizing and progressing an inquiry through to its successful consummation as a contract. Because every professional service company sells efficiency and increased certainty for the client it can, least of all firms, afford to make mistakes, appear dilatory, or disinterested and unreliable.

Thus, the salesman selling professional services has to be both managerial and entrepreneurial—to have and to be seen to have the stature to deal on an equal level to those with whom he must negotiate in the prospect company.

How do they sell?
There are many more ways of selling than by a foot in the door and the product pushed unceremoniously under the prospect's nose. From the very gentle 'concept selling'—that is, putting forward the idea of a service to solve a problem, but not suggesting that the service firm necessarily undertakes the work—to the aggressive 'free trial offer' such as is not unknown in at least one branch of management consultancy for small companies, the range is wide and the nuances infinite.

The method of selling to be adopted will be dependent upon a number of factors:

1 how the inquiry originated—customer-stimulated or service firm-stimulated;
2 type of buying situation—straight rebuy, modified rebuy, new buy;
3 stage of the buying process reached—recognition or anticipation of the problem, determination of and description of characteristics of the need, search for supply source, call for tender, evaluation of tender, selection and order routine;
4 extent of information the client can and is prepared to provide;
5 degree of buying expertise of the client.

Despite the fact that selling professional services still has a large element of a personal *tour de force* or of the artistic virtuoso performance, a careful inspection of successful performances will show that their merit lies in developing the approach in accordance with the principles enunciated in chapter 3, 'The Basic Concepts in Marketing Professional Services', namely, reducing uncertainty, understanding problems, combining professionalism with salesmanship.

To achieve a sale, whether product or service is immaterial, a situation must exist in which the buyer agrees that:

(a) a need exists;
(b) the service offered is the correct one to meet it;
(c) the service company is capable of providing the required service;
(d) the price is acceptable;
(e) the time for completion is satisfactory.

In a straight rebuy situation, it is virtually taken for granted that all points are agreed, although it is recognized that (d) and (e) can alter from purchase to purchase.

In a modified rebuy and new buy situation, the onus is on the seller of services to convince the would-be buyer that all items from (a) to (e) will meet the buying situation requirements.

Just as it is possible to delineate the major points with which a buyer must agree before a sale can be made, so it is possible to define the various steps which the seller must take to achieve this agreement.[1]

- Pre-approach: advance preparation and planning of the sales call.
- Approach: introduction, greeting, appearance, attitude, poise, and mood. A show of enthusiasm and a businesslike manner will favourably impress any prospective client.
- Attention: obtaining undivided and favourable attention. The prospective buyer needs to be convinced that the salesman has a message of importance to him.
- Interest: communicating what the salesman has to sell in terms of the buyer's interests and the benefits to the buyer. This is intrinsic selling.
- Need: presentation of benefits in a deliberate, clear, relevant, and skilful manner.
- Favourable decision: logical summarization of the most convincing arguments, partly developed from the preceding dialogue.

The fundamental distinctions which must be considered in a sales situation were set out in chapter 3. The first of these is the extrinsic/intrinsic method of selling.[2] The desideratum is always to sell intrinsically if the situation will permit this, and the prospective client will respond to such an approach because he appreciates its inherent value over extrinsic selling. However, in most situations, the selling position will be a mix of both intrinsic and extrinsic approaches, and only the sensitivity and understanding of the seller

[1] W K Steinkamp, *How to Sell and Market Industrial Products*. Chilton (Philadelphia, 1970). P. 25 *et al.*
[2] Warren J Wittreich, 'How to Buy/Sell Professional Services', *Harvard Business Review* (Cambridge, Mass., March/April 1961).

for the situation and the personalities of the people involved will tell him the correct mix (see Figure 7.1, page 70).

There may, of course, be no decision to make if the potential buyer only wishes to know what the service firm can do for him without volunteering what it wants it to do, or circumstances surrounding the buying situation. Equally, the decision as between intrinsic and extrinsic selling may be made unconsciously and in response to the dialogue which ensues between buyer and seller. There are no set formulae on how to sell that can be adopted, even if the precise situation relating to the headings given is known. A knowledge of the factors on page 99—(1) how the inquiry originated, (2) type of buying situation, and (3) stage of the buying process reached—will provide a very precise and accurate guide to the salesman for developing his sales approach.

As soon as the seller must decide, whether consciously or unconsciously, what combination of intrinsic/extrinsic selling is required, the second series of distinctions described in chapter 3 is called into consideration. These are the three approaches: *persuasion by method, persuasion by personnel*, and *persuasion by success story*. It has already been pointed out that selling extrinsically represents a less than satisfactory approach, but that this is a position which many who market professional services are forced into by the refusal or inability of the client, at least at the outset, to give him the material from which he can sell 'inwards'. Thus, it is important to understand the three approaches and to use them to open up the situation which enables the seller to initiate or revert to the more efficient intrinsic selling. The three methods of persuasion are thus routes to a buyer-seller relationship from which the main selling effort can be made.

The first of these, *persuasion by method*, is a technique by which the characteristic of the service is sold rather than its consequences. Nowhere is this better illustrated than in current practices in marketing research. Here, sellers concentrate on how the data will be obtained and not how they can be used. Techniques receive all the emphasis and marketing research gets bought by the pound.

Logically, business problem-solving should come first and methods of solving them only second. In professional service selling, as illustrated in the marketing research example, precisely the opposite occurs and as a result business situations are often distorted to meet techniques available. For example, a manufacturer of industrial cleaning materials able to obtain initial business, but having difficulty in acquiring repeat orders, found, in seeking assistance, that the situation was interpreted by different professional service providers as a sales force, a product, an administration, an R & D, an advertising, and a logistic problem. Each interpretation reflected the special expertise of the service company consulted.

Nevertheless, with the salesman emphasizing the methodological approach, provided it is stress on flexibility and not a fixation on methodology, there is at least a basis for coming to grips with substantive problems. The salesman must make it clear that the methods to be adopted are dependent on the nature of the situation; the purchaser must then describe the problem, if there is to be a realistic basis on which to assess the service being sold. This has the double advantage of helping both to identify the problem correctly and the professional who can recognize the limits of his knowledge and skill.

The second technique adopted to emphasize the 'plus' of the professional service firm is *persuasion by personnel*. The reputation and experience of key personnel are major assets of a professional service firm, but unless the client can understand how a solid reputation will translate into specific benefits, it has little real relevance other than providing a certain level of credibility for the company. Moreover, when a client is not talking directly with the personnel whose services are being marketed, he has little opportunity of assessing for himself those whose reputation is supposed to impress him.

There are, of course, a number of circumstances in which persuasion by personnel makes sense. Although outstanding knowledge of the customer company's technology, techniques or organization are not always required to solve a problem, the existence on the staff of an acknowledged leading expert contributes not only to credibility, but also towards the removal of some of the initial uncertainties. However, even in these circumstances, the representative of the service firm must have a demonstrable knowledge and skill in the claimed area of competence.

The third technique is that of *persuasion by success story*, and is the one most likely to succeed if handled tactfully and purposefully, but more often than not it defeats its own purpose because the analogy is not appropriate. This is because the buyer's situation is not understood. The emphasis must be less on the success story than on the substantive nature of the problem. Explaining a success does not necessarily convince the potential buyer of the service that an element of luck did not exist on that occasion, that the situation would have resolved itself anyway, that a combination of factors besides the activities of the professional service firm were at work. By stressing the substantive nature of the problem and the specific skills used to interpret and solve it, two things are achieved:

- the buyer is able to assess the service firm's capabilities in recognizing a unique aspect of a given situation, and
- an evaluation is permitted of the firm's capabilities in coming to grips with the problem.

In other words, in the use of an analogy, the buyer must be capable of identifying himself with the situation being described.

An interesting example of failing to come to grips with a problem is quoted by Edward Hodnett.[1]

[1] E Hodnett, *Effective Presentations*. Parker (West Nyack, N.Y. 1967). Pp. 56–57.

The advertising manager of a hospital supplies firm decides to do an educational film on viruses. He wants it to be educational, not commercial. He hopes it will combine scientific and artistic excellence. He gets in touch with three film producers, explains his aims, and invites them to visit his company's headquarters and make their presentations.

All three follow exactly the same faulty tactics. They show films that have no scientific elements and only routine photographic interest. They talk for a couple of hours about their organization, equipment, and creative talent. They assert that, although they have no knowledge of viruses, they can pick up enough knowledge in a short time to make a film about any subject. . . . The advertising manager is listening for one message—what they can do to make a scientific film about viruses that will meet his criteria. The film producers do not make a sale because they never send the message he is listening for.

This is a typical example of a failure to sell by success story, the use of an inappropriate analogy. The correct use of the approach is illustrated by a marketing consultancy company asked to advise on diversification opportunities in a service activity—employment agencies and executive search. Having obtained an understanding of the inquirer's operations and of the problem, the consultant compared it with work which had been completed for another type of service company—a telephone rental firm. He pointed out that the major strengths of the latter company were, on investigation, found to be considerable skills in branch office operation and financial transactions, not, as that company at first thought, superior equipment and sales force. The solution of the rental company problem was based on the exploitation of these skills using other types of hardware than telephone systems.

The employment agency having a large number of branch offices could immediately see the relevance of the analogy to their own position. Moreover, balancing financial resources—borrowing to finance production and repayment over time—was not so dissimilar as balancing supply of temporary labour with demand. The solution to the telephone rental company's problem of diversification, while being dissimilar to the employment agency's, did indicate a successful approach which had an immediate and easily perceived relevance. The message the potential buyer was listening for came across clearly—the consultant had indicated by reference to past success and appropriate analogies that he could assist him.

When do they sell?
Selling professional services is an on-going process, and there is, as Wittreich points out, no single point in the course of a relationship with a client when the sale is made, but there are many points in that relationship where effective selling is required. Moreover, the sale is not complete until the project is completed to the client's satisfaction.[1]

This is the 'creeping commitment' rather than the 'moment of truth' described in chapter 5, 'The Selection of a Professional Service Company',

[1] Warren J Wittreich, *Selling—A Prerequisite to Success as a Professional*. (A paper presented at a conference in Detroit, Mich., 8 January 1969.)

which can be analysed aside from the problem context and the environment which gave rise to it. Realistically, it is the decision-making *process*, not the decision, which governs the speed, timing, and sequence of the selling effort.

'The decision-making process for most professional services involves a series of incremental choices, each of which eliminates certain alternative solutions from further consideration. As each successive decision is made, the number of possible alternatives is reduced.'[1] The buying process, as delineated in Figure 5.1, page 49, is along a continuum; the selling process must follow that same continuum which is illustrated in Figure 7.1, page 70, where the various selling approaches and marketing activities are shown in a matrix alongside the buying stages.

From this, it will be seen that personal selling, unlike all the other marketing functions, can, and usually is, involved during the whole buying process. A great deal will depend, of course, on whether an inquiry is customer- or service-firm-inspired, since in the former case the second stage—anticipation or recognition of need—will have already taken place, and in all probability attitudes will have been formed on the third stage—assessment of service characteristics needed—and fourth stage—definition of characteristics of service needed.

The actual timing of personal selling activities can be considered under six separate, but interlinked, activities which are roughly chronological in order.

1 Group communications. This entails exposing the prospective clients as a group to the services provided by the professional firm. Although this is frequently achieved by advertising, there is a very definite place in group communications for the salesman. Because, as has already been noted, personal selling is flexible and comprehensive, it is possible to refine the sales message to meet the needs of a particular group. In-plant and public seminars, luncheon meetings, presentations both at the service firm and on the client's premises, are all effective sales techniques.

Although in group communications there must be a larger element of extrinsic selling than in individual communication, it is still perfectly feasible to narrow down the sales approach to encompass the interest of the individual firm and its departments.

In, for example, the presentation of a corporate long-range planning service to a group of executives within a chemical manufacturing concern, the first stress would be placed on the relevance of the service to a chemical manufacturer and on that part of the output of the service which is concerned with chemicals and technologies impacting on them. At this point, the intrinsic approach can be mixed with the extrinsic approach by *selling by personnel* and stressing the capabilities of the staff of the service in chemicals and related

[1] P J Robinson *et al., Industrial Buying and Creative Marketing.* Allyn & Bacon (Boston, Mass., 1967). P. 19.

fields. It is then possible to pinpoint certain specific audiences in the company and how this service will be of use to them. Corporate management, who must make the plans, will derive benefit from the information on techniques the service provides to assist the development of planning strategies and methodologies. Operating management, who must implement the plans made by corporate management, would be assisted by the very practical instructional courses and manuals provided as part of the service. Research and development would be able to tap into the technical monitoring service which examines the impacts of changing technologies on each other and on product and process development. Marketing research will receive its benefit from the flow of commercial information and forecasts on markets, industries, products, and applications.

Thus, a group communication process can use both intrinsic and extrinsic methods and can achieve a number of objectives, one of which will be to lead on to a meeting with the decision-makers in the purchase of the service, perhaps the corporate planning manager and finance director.

2 Individual communications. It is obvious that the major selling effort will not begin until the decision-makers, at each stage of the selection process, are identified and the salesmen are interacting with the potential clients on an individual basis to obtain an understanding of the client's perspectives, problems, attitudes, and organization. It is only at this stage that the raw material for intrinsic selling can be obtained and hence the feedback which is vital for the successful accomplishment of the remainder of the selling effort.

Selling on an individual basis more than any other marketing activity will highlight the problem of antipathy to selling experienced by many professional people, since not all contacts will be at the client's request, nor the ground prepared for the meeting. 'Cold calling', under some circumstances, may be necessary, and may be regarded by many professionals engaged in selling as impertinent, undignified, and aggressive. Cold calling in professional service selling is not usual, but something very close to it is, namely, telephoning or writing to seek a meeting with the identified decision-maker. Unless a good reason can be advanced for a request for such a meeting, it is likely to be rejected, something professionals find particularly unpleasant. It is necessary, therefore, to express the reason for a meeting in terms of advantage to the client. Unfortunately, the most aggressive types of life insurance selling have inspired a very predictable response, unless the reason can be seen to be more specific than 'it would be to your benefit'.

To ease the task of opening up the route for a face-to-face meeting, it is important for the salesman to obtain as much advance information as possible about the company and the person to be seen. He must decide on how he will identify himself and his company and, most important of all, how he will express his purpose for seeking a meeting. Moreover, the salesman should consider what reasons may be advanced for refusing a meeting so that he can be ready to counter them. The opening statement to the prospective client is vital. It should be prepared, rehearsed, and tested.

One other consideration requires mention. It is not always possible to make direct contact with the person to be seen. A layer, or several layers, of 'screening' personnel may stand between the salesman and the target. The task of getting to the required person may well be complicated by the 'screens'; the information presented to them may have to differ from that which would be given to the decision-maker directly if only to avoid pre-emption of the conversation and a refusal at the wrong level against which there can be no appeal.

Thus, the tactics to be adopted in the event of screening personnel refusing a meeting must be decided in advance, and this can only be done if some appreciation is gained of what reasons they are likely to advance for refusal. Thus, all refusals and objections should be carefully analysed. It is, of course, additionally useful to know if the reasons screening personnel give for a refusal will be the same as those advanced by the target personnel themselves. Even if they are, it does not imply that the counter arguments for each group will be the same.

For example, the request for a meeting to discuss information retrieval and abstracting services might be refused by the librarian on the grounds that the library is capable of undertaking this work themselves. The service seller would need to explain how the service, possessing as it does a far wider range of skills and capabilities (e.g., language, technical qualifications) than even the best equipped commercial library, can extend the reach of the library and the librarian and improve its services to the company as a whole. If, however, the meeting was refused by the head of internal services, an explanation may be needed in terms of cost effectiveness, speed or accuracy of the service, or access to sources not available to the company librarian.

Meetings with screening personnel can, however, have a positive advantage in that they can be used to put fact-finding questions concerning the firm and the decision-makers, the answers to which will assist in the ultimate presentation.

Finally, although it may appear to be a trivial point, the salesman must be able to meet, within reason, any suggested time, date, and place for a meeting offered. Thus it is unwise for the salesman to seek interviews with a fairly full appointment diary.

3 *Identification of opportunities.* The whole of chapter 8, 'Identifying Market Opportunities', has been devoted to this subject. Both client-generated and service company-generated inquiries require that the sales opportunity, once identified, should be related to the ability of the service company to meet the real needs of the situation, which, in turn, implies that the salesman's ability to interpret the needs of the prospect must be of a high order of professionalism and integrity.

4 Presentation of the service offer. If there were a 'moment of truth' in professional servicing purchasing, it would be at this point. If it is on a personal level, the offer will require all the skills of presentation as well as those of salesmanship.

The technical and mechanical aspects demand as much care as the message to be conveyed. Thus, the presentation must follow a logical pattern: perhaps the background to the raising of the inquiry, a statement of the problem or original situation analysis, restatement in terms of the problem isolated as critical, detailed description of the approach and methodology, the total expected yield from the application of the service to the situation, and expression of the solution in terms of personal and/or corporate benefits to be obtained. Again, it must be emphasized that the buyer is listening for one thing only: 'What will the purchase of this service do for me?'

The presentation must be at a level which is compatible with the state of knowledge of the listener and this obviously affects the form and content of the presentation. The less familiar the listener is with the subject matter, the greater the uncertainty he will exhibit. Thus, the salesman needs to develop a mental scale of the 'state of knowledge':

- ignorant (of the subject matter);
- below average;
- average;
- above average;
- expert.

A presentation which has misjudged the state of knowledge by more than one category has every likelihood of failing both as a presentation and in its objectives to achieve some predetermined action.

Thus, if a presentation is pitched at 'average' level to a group of experts, it will be largely wasted and will result in impatience, aggression, and even ridicule. An above average level of presentation to a below average audience will not achieve an understanding, and without understanding they would be foolish to take any action. Moreover, to reveal, however unwittingly, the lack of knowledge of the audience, is hardly likely to produce a favourable atmosphere.

One of the obvious and fundamental differences in service as opposed to product selling is the lack of anything tangible to show or demonstrate. But while it is not possible to show a professional service, it is certainly possible to develop visual material to illustrate the outcome of the application of the service to the situation.

Indeed, it is more important in presenting an offer of professional services to produce visual material than in a product selling situation where even if the product cannot be shown at the meeting, it can be produced at some time or in some location. Thus, the professional service salesman should seek some visual means of demonstrating his services, but they must not be contrived. A checklist for the use of visual material might be devised:

- Is the point worth making?
- Can it be adequately verbalized—if so, what purpose would visualization achieve?
- Does the visual aid supplement the verbal medium rather than replace it?
- Does the visual achieve unity?
- Are the symbols acceptable?
- Is it visually fluent?
- Is the visual honest?
- Does it utilize all available techniques to improve its effectiveness?
- Is the visual for the benefit of the audience or the presenter?
- Is it readable by all those present?

Not every salesman of professional services is capable of developing his own visual aids to his presentation. There are, however, within many service firms, departments and individuals who can supply this facility, and, in any event, there are professional firms specializing in the preparation of visual aids.

At the presentation, the salesman is faced with showing the relevance and cost effectiveness of the service he offers to the specific problem identified. He must ensure that the would-be client is satisfied that the correct service is being offered and that the most suitable professionals will be allocated to the work. The total offer must meet, to the maximum extent possible, the fundamental needs of the client: reduction of uncertainty in both the situation to be resolved and in the selection and commissioning of the service; confidence that the problem has been understood; and assurance that the professionalism of the service company is of the highest order.

5 *Monitoring.* During the execution of the service, there should be a constant feedback to client management on the progress and results. Although this may well be a function of the professionals actually undertaking the work, there is a strong case for it being undertaken by the man who sold the assignment, alone or in cooperation with the professionals. Because service projects will sometimes change during their execution, without good communication and feedback the areas of uncertainty can widen and become more, not less, intense. Expectations have an unpredictable habit of moving out of line with reality. By monitoring the situation, the salesman can avoid client disappointment and frustration at the end of the project and ensure continuing goodwill.

Monitoring can only be successfully achieved if both good working relations and good communications are established between the client and the service company. These desiderata call for a clear understanding of the role of each party, something the salesman can help to achieve, standing as he does between the professionals who do the work and the client who will be the recipient of the result. Agreement is needed as to whom letters, communications, and reports must be addressed, and with whom meetings can be held. A large part of setting up an effective communication system will be the responsibility of the professionals assigned to the project, but the salesman has a role to play in ensuring that a system *is* set up and maintained. Such a system MUST include the salesman, so that he is always aware of the situation on the assignment he sold, and can report back knowledgeably to the client. Bearing in mind that the salesman will, by choice, be a professional who can sell and will thus have the confidence of both the professional on the job and the client, he is, indeed, in an ideal position to monitor and report on progress. Monitoring arrangements make an important contribution to stable operating conditions, and are thus an integral part of the selling process.

6 Follow-through. It has already been pointed out in chapter 4, 'The Buying/ Selling Interface', that just as the delivery of a product is not necessarily the end of the supplier's involvement, neither is the end of the service contract the end of an involvement. Producers of professional services are strategically placed to watch the outcome of their work, but frequently fail to do so. Setting aside the fact that interest shown in a client's performance following completion of a service project is an affirmation of the service company's faith in its own work, it is also indicative of commitment and acceptance of responsibility. Moreover, 'following through' is an indication of professionalism and at the same time provides opportunities for appraising new service needs. Thus, the salesman can achieve the double objective of continuing to reduce uncertainty and inspire confidence in his client while having the opportunity of assessing new potentials for business within the client firm.

The selling phases described, although parallel with the buying phases, are not mutually exclusive. Thus the 'follow-through' process contains many of the elements of the 'individual communication' phases.

Profile of a professional who can sell
The seller of professional services will tend, rightly, to regard himself as a manager of his own personal service business. He sees himself in two roles: to help his clients maximize the profitable operation of their business and, thereby, to maximize the profitable operation of his own business. He is concerned with the sum total of his clients' needs which his combined professional and corporate expertise can help make more efficient or economic.

Additionally, because the seller of professional services is managerial or entrepreneurial, he concentrates on profitable sales, not just on selling more. To do so, however, he has to have a degree of personal security in relationships with, and an understanding of, his firm, to hold their confidence, and to be able to know and understand what constitutes a 'profitable sale'.

The seller of professional services is essentially a planner, because he plans not only the individual calls, but also his entire business relationship with his clients. 'The process of long-range profit planning is the turnkey even in the consultative salesman's client relationships, since it is through his planning partnership with his clients that he embeds himself and his product-service systems into his client's business.'[1] This statement refers to the selling of consultative services as part of a product sale, but is also apposite to the selling of professional services as an activity in its own right.

Finally, the seller of professional services is an innovator. He seeks out needs for new services and new markets and actively presides over combined client-supplier approaches to anticipating these needs and the means of satisfying them. The work and attributes of the professional service salesman have been summed up.[2]

- performs a long-term business planning function for his customer-clients and for their own key customers;
- helps customer-clients define their businesses, their markets, and their product-service systems;
- maintains wide, multi-function access inside client companies and with their own key customers;
- sells systems of services;
- draws on the full complement of his company's functions and services for his support.

The salesman has the responsibility of closing the client-service firm communication loop as a marketing-oriented activity, but he and his company must recognize that the actual buying and selling of professional services is only one significant part of the total marketing effort in which he and they must be engaged.

[1] Mack Hanan, James Cribbin, and Herman Heiser, *Consultative Selling*. American Management Association (New York, 1970). P. 13.
[2] Ibid., p. 14.

11

Marketing functions:
Non-personal promotion

The non-personal communication processes in marketing are often subject to misunderstanding by sponsors, practitioners, and recipients of the message. This is because of the confusion which frequently exists between methods and media, and the lack of any precise agreed objective for the promotional activity.

The range of methods and media might appear to be limited so far as services are concerned, and even more limited for professional services both because of the ethical considerations (real or imagined) already referred to, or because of the professional's perception of himself, his services, and his customers. Many professionals ask how the communications process can be carried out consistently and efficiently without breaching the ethical barriers or laws of their profession, while at the same time not falling back on the vagaries of referals or just *laissez-faire*.

Many methods of promotion are written off prematurely as inapplicable or too brash for professional services, but conditions of market leadership are established either by doing uncommonly well that which is commonly done or doing that which is uncommon. In the context of professional services, it is the latter approach which offers the best opportunities. The marketing man must ensure that:

- promotional methods are clearly defined and agreed;
- targets are identified and are practical;
- the message conveyed is effective;
- coordination is achieved;
- feedback occurs;
- evaluation, even if only in approximate terms, is possible.

Thus, among the early questions which require answers are:

- What coverage is needed?
- What frequency must be adopted?

● What continuity is necessary?

If objectives and targets are precise, the coordination of these three aspects will ensure that promotion is not undertaken on a hit and miss or reactive basis. Indeed, one of the commonest failings of service firms is the sudden termination of all promotional activities in response to their success. That is, a high workload leads to reduced or cancelled promotion.

It is as well, perhaps, to briefly examine the communication process in order to understand the role of persuasive and informative messages of any type and disseminated by any method or media.

The prospective buyer of any service must be taken through the series of steps represented in Figure 11.1 by the horizontal bars and under the impetus of marketing forces which, in turn, are resisted by countervailing pressures.[1]

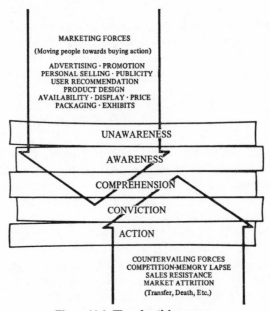

Figure 11.1. The advertising process

The stronger the market forces, the more quickly will the prospective buyer be moved towards the decision. Conversely, the strength of the counter-vailing forces will move him further from the decision.

This is the communications process in all marketing, not just the marketing of services. The variations will only be in emphasis and method—strident for domestic consumables, subtle and esoteric for the senior professions of medicine and law.

[1] A H Colley, 'Squeezing the Waste Out of Advertising', *Harvard Business Review* (Cambridge, Mass., September/October 1962).

112

Appropriation setting

Appropriation setting for non-personal promotion is a most difficult task and involves problems not adequately solved in any area of marketing. 'Rule of thumb' methods tend to be applied and, while they may be helpful in some circumstances, they can be totally misleading, ineffective, or even disastrous in others.

Three approaches which avoid the 'rule of thumb' method are applicable to some types of services. The incremental method assigns a unit cost of advertising to each unit sold. For example, £10 of advertising appropriation might be allowed for each £1000 of the unit sold. This method can only be applied to standardized services, for instance, some types of insurance and banking. It is totally inappropriate for 'one-off' problem-solving services, such as those involved in contract R & D and management consultancy.

The incremental and percentage of sales method treats advertising as a variable or semi-variable sales cost. Additional expenditures of advertising are made on a per unit increment assignment or on a percentage of total revenues. This is little more than 'rule of thumb' using x per cent of sales which takes no cognizance of the marketing strategy and targets, and is governed either by past performance or projections of present performance. It is thus reactive rather than deliberate.

Another method which has gained acceptance is the objective-and-task method. The objectives of the programme are set out and the cost to attain them estimated and then budgeted. If a ratio of advertising to net profits can be obtained either from published data or interfirm comparisons, it is possible to use this as the basis. It cannot, of course, be claimed that there is a causal relationship between net profits and advertising, but the fact that some relationship exists provides a tool to use as an aid to judgement.

The advantage of the objective-and-task method is that it forces attention on objective setting and on the roles to be played by different types of promotion, it encourages detailed planning by each section of the firm, it is based on a philosophy of what is needed as opposed to availability of funds, and it facilitates measurement and evaluation.[1]

By using the objective-and-task method, the appropriation is built up from a summation of needs for each element in the communication mix, so that in deciding the global appropriation the functional ones are decided, too.

For professional service companies, the choice of methods and media is relatively limited, and, thus, the task will be less difficult and onerous than conducting the same exercise for consumer goods and services.

Promotional goals

The need for unambiguous objectives for the marketing strategy has been emphasized. The requirement is no less for the marketing functions, particularly for professional services in which so many of the marketing techniques

[1] H R Dodge, *Industrial Marketing*. McGraw-Hill (New York, 1970). Pp. 354–356.

have yet to be accepted as appropriate (this applies particularly to non-personal promotion).

Figure 11.2 illustrates some promotional objectives, methods, and media, and shows that the range of possibilities is far greater than might be supposed from a superficial consideration of promotion in relation to professional services. Obviously not all alternatives are listed, nor are all those listed necessarily applicable to all services, but a sufficient number is included to suggest that the marketing man in professional services can safely widen his horizons and increase the number of options open to him in presenting his service to actual and prospective clients.

Four principal methods of promotion are considered in this chapter: press advertising, PR (public relations), direct mail, and merchandising techniques.

Press advertising

Whereas for products, press advertising almost invariably accounts for the bulk of the appropriation expenditure, in services of all types, not only professional services, press advertising rarely represents a substantial part of the promotion appropriation, and even more rarely of the total marketing costs. Nevertheless, it has been commented that, in general, the principles and practices of advertising and sales promotion are similar for the marketing of goods as for services. If this is true, it would appear that the major reason accounting for the differences in emphasis between goods and services media appropriation is the difficulty of attempting to convey the coverage, quality, and depth of a service in written or illustrated form. The basic problem with media advertising of services is their very intangibility. The services have to be made visually attractive—no easy thing to achieve—which explains the preference in many service firms for alternative forms of promotion.

The extent to which media advertising (press, outdoor, direct mail, etc.) can be used effectively depends entirely upon the extent to which the service can be promoted in non-verbal terms. It is relatively easy for a hotel to advertise its services through the use of pictures of the hotel and its environment, while the travel agent is thrown back on symbols of travel such as aeroplanes, ships, and city logos. Not even reference to the degree of tangibility (see Figure 1.2, page 8) gives a clue as to the appropriateness of media advertising in any particular circumstance, since a pure intangible, such as communication systems, can be illustrated more effectively in print than, for example, a service making a tangible available, such as factoring.

The rules for effective and efficient use of advertising have been set out in numerous publications and textbooks, but none has managed—nor it would seem is ever likely to manage—to convey the means by which high attention-getting, attractive, and economic advertising can be created to order. The act of creativity is not easily analysed, although it does not mean to say it cannot be structured to some extent.

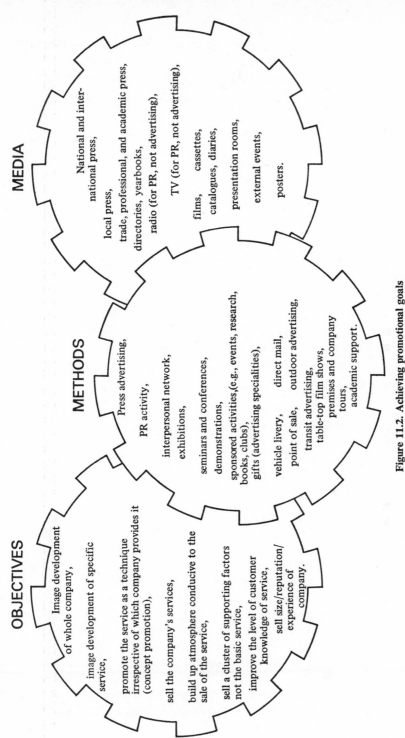

Figure 11.2. Achieving promotional goals

115

Rodger has commented[1] that the idea of the creative advertising man sitting at a typewriter or drawing board, pen or brush in hand, working to an open-sky brief and waiting for inspiration to strike is far removed from the truth.

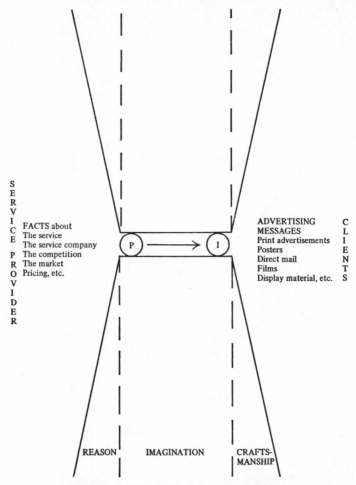

Figure 11.3. The creative process in advertising

The fundamental starting point of any advertisement must be the realization that it is a communication process between two people—the supplier on the one hand and the customer on the other. It has been visualized in Figure 11.3, although 'services' have been substituted for 'manufacturers'.[2]

Creativity starts with the purchasing proposition (P) in Figure 11.3, and seeks to find an original advertising idea which best expresses and *communicates* the proposition. The purchasing proposition becomes an original

[1] Leslie Rodger, *Marketing in a Competitive Economy.* Associated Business Programmes (London, 1971). P. 203.
[2] Ibid.

advertising idea (I), through the application of insight and imagination. It is turned into the physical advertisement by skilled craftsmen (not the do-it-yourself all-purpose service marketer). Rodger's view on the essential similarity of most products is equally appropriate to many professional services, namely:

> Relatively so few products are demonstrably and obviously superior to anything else on the market that the problem more often than not is one of communicating significant product differences rather than major, perhaps unique, product advantages. Hence differences between essentially similar products sharing the same basic purchase proposition will often depend upon unique creative interpretation of the proposition.[1]

For service as opposed to product markets, the essential difference lies in the first few words of the statement, 'are demonstrably . . . superior'. If it is difficult to demonstrate the superiority of a physical purchase, the problem is many times compounded with a service by the fact that what is advertised is intangible—a concept, a benefit, a promise.

As a result, advertising of services tends to be 'wordy', whereas the message should be unambiguous and a simple presentation of the information needed for each type of decision. Clearly, it is easier to stipulate than to achieve this requirement. Given the difficulty of doing this, then advertising must seek, through a clear theme, colour, and design, to project the image of the service and its provider in those markets which are attracted by visual presentation.

It has already been shown that advertising to succeed *must get attention*. A close knowledge of the market, and of the attitudes and practices prevailing within it, is necessary to ensure that attention-getting qualities of advertising will have a positive, favourable effect. The professional service company must be able to identify the appeals which will attract attention and are convincing. *The emphasis should be placed on the utilities and customer benefits of the services rather than on the technical details which may not be related to the satisfaction of customer needs and desires.*

Given that the would-be buyer of professional services can only rarely use his own expertise to assess the claims made by a professional service company in advance of its performance, as opposed to the way in which a buyer of a product can often judge its likely performance characteristics, the advertising must rest strongly on the *promise* of the performance and the benefits which will ensue. Emphasizing *promise*, however, has its dangers since it draws attention to the essentially intangible nature of the purchase, the difficulty of ascertaining if the correct service and the right practitioner have been chosen, and, above all, of determining if value for money will be or has been obtained. Thus, for advertisers of services, the appeal tends, for lack of a better alternative, to rest on creating awareness and emphasizing the attraction of the service to the target user groups in terms of the benefits to be obtained. 'The features of the service must be translated into powerful benefits which will appeal to the reader of the advertising message. Advan-

[1] Ibid.

tages may be stated positively or negatively. A positive appeal is one which promises something the consumer (user) wants. A negative appeal promises a way to avoid something unpleasant.'[1]

There are many widely divergent views as to the number of appeals each advertisement should contain. A single 'plus' is favoured for media, where the study of an advertisement may be only brief and superficial, but several appeals may be equally applicable even in these circumstances, since different buyers with different requirements may find different attractions and each will see what he wishes to see in the advertisement. It is relevant to emphasize again that each buyer is listening for only one message: 'What's in it for me?'

Powerful arguments can be advanced both for and against single or multiple appeals. The decision must be taken on the basis of the advertisement targets, the media chosen, and the frequency adopted. As a general guide for services, one or two major 'plusses' will tend to be sufficient for a single advertisement. A series of advertisements can be used if there are many other benefits to be explained. However, there is nothing dogmatic, nor can there ever be, about approaches to advertising.

In the final analysis, it will probably be the substance of the message conveyed that will be more important than the detail. Clearly, all advertising must be geared to the images the firm wishes to project: this desideratum must never be ignored. The advertising objective may be instant recall of the advertiser's name, but it must be recall which is linked conclusively with the level and quality of service offered.

PR (Public Relations)

Even the most enthusiastic writers on PR admit that it and its practitioners are not well regarded among managers.

> The public relations executive is open to much misdirected criticism.[2]
>
> Their work is frequently misunderstood and they are accused of 'bending the news' and a mean impression of public relations is held by management.[3]
>
> Many people are sceptical and even suspicious of it and the men and women who practise it.[4]

Inevitably *sartor resartus* springs to mind. If the practitioners of this particular professional service are unable to produce a satisfactory image for themselves, how can they produce if for others? But the same criticism can be made of marketing researchers who rarely know how big their own market is, management consultants whose internal communications are chaotic, and, of course, doctors—'Physician heal thyself'.

[1] L H Hodges and R Tillman, *Bank Marketing: Texts and Cases.* Addison-Wesley (Reading, Mass., 1968).
[2] Leslie Rodger, *Marketing in a Competitive Economy.* Associated Business Programmes (London, 1971).
[3] John Winkler, *Marketing for the Developing Company.* Hutchinson (London, 1969).
[4] Harry Trigg, 'Industrial Public Relations', *The Marketing of Industrial Products.* Aubrey Wilson, ed. Pan Books (London, 1972).

The problem in each case rests squarely on the lack of image sensitivity of the practitioners, who so often fail to see how their own internal performance and conditions contribute to the confidence build-up so necessary in buying professional services. This, combined with the deeply-held belief that they are at least as expert in marketing as in the subject of their professionalism, forms a toxic combination for the effective murder of good PR and, thus, good marketing.

The marketing of professional services requires the use of the full range of public relations techniques, if only because for the professional service firm PR with its indirect appeals seems to offer the one reasonably certain way of overcoming embargoes which are maintained for ethical or other reasons on the use of advertising and other promotional methods.

It is not particularly helpful to generalize about the communication mix, since each type of professional service will have widely differing needs, but, by and large, professional service firms will tend to lean more heavily on public and press relations than on press advertising, and will almost totally exclude some types of promotion, such as outdoor and vehicle livery. That this is so, and is moreover a correct approach, is borne out by an old but nevertheless still valid study of the influence of word of mouth (or interpersonal network) advertising.[1] The high rate of referals as a source of business in professional services reflects the importance of the interpersonal network. Public relations are far more likely to have an impact on this network than other forms of promotion, hence the selection of PR as the prime method of promotion is a natural corollary of the phenomenon of referals which professional service companies have always been aware of and have always sought to influence.

It is unfortunate that, in marketing terms, the initials PR can stand equally for 'public relations' or 'press relations'. The difference between the two is not just semantic: public relations are concerned with 'the deliberate, planned, and sustained effort to establish and maintain mutual understanding between an organization and its public'.[2] It is a methodical attempt to promote *all* company activities and interests in every way possible (excluding paid advertisements). Press relations are the relatively narrow area of seeking editorial or news column mention in press, radio, or television media, and by definition exclude, for example, special events, exhibitions, conferences, symposia, annual reports, and sponsored books. In the context of this chapter, PR is used to denote public relations unless it is stated to the contrary.

For the professional service firm, most of the PR effort tends to centre on press relations to the neglect of other media, and the mechanics are geared to press needs. Thus, the publicity effort is inhibited from the start.

Public relations cover five aspects of marketing communication:

[1] E Katz and P Lazarsfeld, *Personal Influence*. Free Press (Glencoe, Ill., 1955).
[2] Institute of Public Relations (London).

- client relations;
- industry relations;
- community relations;
- staff relations;
- shareholder relations.

Good client PR, apart from the obvious need to communicate important aspects of the company's performance and activities, include such minute details as training telephone operators and secretaries to be polite, friendly, and helpful, prompt responses to requests for information, and prompt thanks for business and outside cooperation.

Industry relations involve the interaction of the service company with industry or other groups. This includes participation in their own professional activities, such as working parties, study groups, interfirm comparisons, and conferences. Perhaps as important is the provision of speakers at and participation in activities of other groups—professional and non-professional—in which the service company may be interested.

Community relations links the activities of the firm not only to the local community of which it is part, but also to its total environment. The secondment of personnel to sit on official committees (NEDC, BSI), contributions to the state of the arts, assistance to universities and other educational establishments, are all areas of activity for consideration.

Staff relations are concerned internally with personnel factors and externally with recruitment. Well-conceived public relations can do much to enhance employees' sense of pride in the organization's ideals, achievements, growth record, and concepts of service to its clients. In the same manner, PR will considerably aid recruitment of personnel. A high level of awareness concerning the company will have a partial screening effect in attracting applicants conforming more closely to requirements than if knowledge of the organization is lacking or incorrect.

Shareholder relations are directed to developing satisfactory links with shareholders, potential investors, and those who influence investments. The task is not only to keep these audiences informed of the company's achievements and plans, but to ensure that the policies and activities of the company are correctly interpreted.

Since so much depends on the image which the service firm projects, it is perhaps as well to re-examine briefly within the context of PR the question of images and their projection. Images are not merely the concern of PR, but are made and remade by the totality of the company's activities and personnel.

The value of services can be expressed through classical economic theory:

- form utility—the ability of a service to satisfy a need as a result of its structure or composition;
- time utility—the accessibility of a service at a time it is required;

- place utility—the accessibility of a service at a place it is required;
- possession utility—satisfaction resulting from the rendering and receipt of a service.

To this can be added a fifth utility, 'image utility'—the ability of a service to provide satisfaction through the user's perception of the social and personal meanings of the service (in consumer terms) and of the commercial and corporate meanings of the service (in business terms)[1]. It includes all the non-rational satisfactions which a buyer receives, and it explains the success of 'prestige' services, 'traditional' firms, 'in' techniques, 'trendy' solutions.

Studies of buyers' attitudes to their purchases and suppliers has shown that perceptual and conceptual distortion occurs in a significant number of cases, particularly with regard to the images which selling companies and their representatives project Images have taken on a new importance as an appreciation has developed that the crucial factors in many buying situations are the buyer's impressions, not the reality of the firm and its output. Thus, the selling company needs to know not only what image it projects, but also what image is most acceptable to the buyers.

The term 'image' is useful as a shorthand form to describe the external views of individuals or of special publics towards activities, persons, objects, or services. But its popularization has led inevitably to its incorrect use. It has become an omnibus term describing something it was not intended to convey. Moreover, the wrong use of 'image' has led to a belief that under most, if not all, circumstances there is a single image rather than a series. In fact, every investigation has led to the uncovering of a host of images, many contradictory and with infinite shades of meaning to the observers and projectors. Although images are numerous and variable, they can, however, be conveniently grouped:

- *Current image*—how does the outside world see the firm?
- *Mirror image*—how does the company think it is seen to the outside world?
- *Wish image*—how does the company wish to be seen by the outside world?

It requires little imagination to appreciate how these three images can clash. Not quite so obvious is the conflict between the *wish* image, whether translated into action or not, and the image which will produce the best impact on the environment into which it is projected. In other words, the distinction is between how the company wishes to be seen and how it ought to be seen to improve its operations—the *optimum image*.

A further complication is that images of individual firms are usually formed partly by that of their profession as a whole. Thus, the individual

[1] Roman R Andrus, 'Marketing's Other Function,' *The Business Quarterly*. University of Western Ontario (London, Canada, Winter 1968).

firm's *current image* assessment has to be made against an image reference to the profession as a whole.

The research input in an image study is directed towards the identification of an *optimum* image—that is, the most desirable image compatible with the company's policy and long-range objectives. It is with this image that all the others must be brought into focus.

The creation and maintenance of an image is a continuous operation reflecting the pulse beat of the company. Image strategy requires constant supervision and testing because the image changes in response to changes in the environment into which it is projected.

The study of images enables the firm's marketing management to develop two benchmarks. The first is obtained by bringing the *current* and *mirror* images into focus. This will provide a first base from which the image strategy can be launched. The second, which is where internal persuasion is involved, is to bring the *wish* and *optimum* images into focus. This gives the objective for the image strategy, which the company must implement. With these benchmarks the marketing strategists can decide on the most suitable means for reaching the established goal.[1]

As with press and other forms of media advertising, the contribution of PR to the marketing performance is difficult to evaluate, particularly as any results are likely to occur over a period of time considerably greater than that of any particular PR campaign of activity. Because evaluation is difficult, little attempt has been made to quantify both costs and results, and campaigns often lack a structural entity which is so important to avoid self-cancellation and lack of impact.

A useful checklist has been developed by John Winkler to ensure that the PR effort is channelled effectively, that no major groups or steps are omitted, and that the costs involved are known as they occur and can be monitored. Adjusted for professional services, it provides the guidelines shown in Figure 11.4.

Good public relations should be a channel, not a barrier, between the service company and its public. It is a regular continuous programme of sensitive response to the various publics served. It is not a posture of goodwill assumed in order to solve current problems and given up when those problems are removed. Of the many elements in the marketing mix, PR is perhaps the most applicable and powerful available to marketers of professional services. It is the one they must study, understand, and practise, if marketing is to be effective in its totality.

The opportunities for good press and public relations for most service firms are myriad and wasted. This wastage occurs because professionals rarely see the news angle of what the journalists call a 'sexy' story. The do-it-

[1] A full discussion of the multiple image concept will be found in Aubrey Wilson, *The Art and Practice of Marketing*. Hutchinson (London, 1971). Pp. 75–81, and in Aubrey Wilson, *The Assessment of Industrial Markets*. Hutchinson (London, 1968). Pp. 251–253.

Figure 11.4.
PR checklist

1 Company publication

AUDIENCE

External
- User industries, trades, and professions
- Peer groups (own management, influential firms, competitors, government, etc.)
- City and financial institutions
- Shareholders
- Other groups (specify)
- Professional bodies

METHOD

Written word
- Company news. This is a continuous service to all appropriate media
- Feature placing
- Special promotion
- Personality promotion
- Other (specify)

Spoken word
- Talks
- Premises visits/open days
- Films
- Demonstrations
- Other methods (specify)

PRIME MEDIA
- International and regional press
- International and national business papers (specify key publications)
- User press (specify key publications)
- TV and radio
- Direct mail (specify audiences)
- Interpersonal network
- Yearbooks and directories
- Other media (specify)

2 Marketing communications

AUDIENCE

External
- Customers
- Key customers
- Potential customers
- Special interest groups (specify)
- Others (specify)

Internal
- Professional staff
- Sales force
- Management
- Other groups (specify)

METHOD
- News concerning service
- Feature placing
- Service information, brochures, reprints, checklists, case histories
- Promotional schemes, (a) internal, (b) external
- Sales story/sales training
- Newsletter, (a) internal, (b) external
- Hire of special staff
- Sales-briefing (conferences, etc.)
- Control and motivation data
- Lectures, (a) internal, (b) external
- Others (specify)

PRIME MEDIA
- User trade press (specify key publications)
- Direct mail (specify key groups)
- Hand-out material
- Merchandising material
- Sales support material
- Exhibits and demonstrations
- Interpersonal network
- TV, radio, international, and business press
- Advertising (including outdoor)
- Other media (specify)

3 Company/product presentation

AUDIENCE

External
- User groups
- General public
- Peer groups (influence formers, professional bodies)
- City and financial institutions
- Special groups (specify)

Internal
- Staff
- Management
- Visitors
- Others (specify)

METHOD

Design
- Symbol
- Creative format (typography, packaging)
- Technical illustration
- Photography
- Other

Writing
- Writing new material
- Rewriting old material
- Other (specify)

PRIME MEDIA
- Advertising design
- Letterheads, etc.
- Company fascias, etc.
- Sales literature
- Vehicle livery
- Receptionists
- Internal literature
- House journal
- Staff notices
- Reception area
- Presentation rooms
- Others (specify)

4 Community relations

AUDIENCE
- Local community near company offices and part-time and casual staff
- Potential full-time staff (male/female)
- Local commercial interests
- Local authorities
- Local associations (special interest groups)
- Other local groups (specify)

METHOD
- Personnel news service
- Feature placing
- Premises visits for press
- Redesign/rewriting of material
- Reception, recruitment, induction procedure, forms and literature
- Public tours/open days
- Exhibitions/demonstrations
- Professional organizations
- Rotary/Round Table
- Political associations and clubs
- Consumer groups
- Woman's organizations
- Local councillors and MP's
- Ratepayers and other associations
- Other groups

PRIME MEDIA
- Local press
- Regional press/radio/TV
- Advertising, (a) press, (b) other
- Direct mail
- Interpersonal network
- Company fascias
- Other media (specify)

yourself propensity of professional service companies is never exhibited to worse effect than in their clumsy efforts to obtain press or other coverage. Public relations are professional work of a special sort. Professionals ought never to be afraid to employ professionals to undertake specialist activities in which they have no skills or only limited skills.

Direct mail

It has always been recognized that one of the most valuable forms of media for small firms is direct mail, and since most professional services tend to be small, this is a technique which finds favour with them. The medium combines the opportunity for a personal approach with the efficiencies of mass advertising.

The major advantage of direct mail advertising is that it is possible to target the message accurately on the firms and, indeed, on the individual in firms to whom it is directed. It is recognized, however, that many lists on which direct mail campaigns are based are taken from directories and other sources which can be as much as 40 to 50 per cent inaccurate. This is caused by removals, internal changes, mergers, start-ups, and discontinuities. However, such a high order of inaccuracy does not have to be accepted if firms take care in ensuring that the source list is of a reasonably recent date, is a reliable compilation, and that it is 'cleaned' and monitored. But, even on a high wastage rate, direct mail can be economic when the residual contacts provide a high response.

The question of reliability of the sources of addresses is of prime importance. Membership of organizations, shareholders' lists, attendances at conferences, are likely to be accurate at the time of compilation, which is more than can be said for journal circulation lists and many trade directories. Many source lists begin on a false basis in that they claim or imply they are exhaustive when, in fact, a firm appears in them by virtue of having bought the space. The question of topicality is equally important. Local rating lists are reckoned to be 10 per cent out of date at their time of publication, and this is certainly true of yearbooks and other annual publications. Thus, a three-year-old directory could be as much as 30 per cent inaccurate.

With a good base list, it is possible to undertake a certain amount of 'cleaning' from the internal knowledge of the company. For example, in *The Times's* and *Fortune's* lists of leading companies, it is possible without difficulty to identify the major mergers not accounted for in the compilations. Similarly, anyone knowledgeable about advertising could without difficulty separate in any of the many directories firms which concentrate on consumer markets from those that specialize in industrial markets.

Once a good base list is obtained then monitoring should occur as a routine process. This enables changes to be recorded, for example, the appointment of new personnel, changes of address, acquisitions and divestment, and other corporate activities. Given these checks and activities, the direct mail lists can be accurate and therefore at the very least the mailing begins with the possibility of success enhanced.

The second major advantage of direct mail is that it can be controlled in its timing and rate of dispatch to ensure that the advertiser can exploit environmental factors and also cope with the resulting replies. A carefully planned full page advertisement in the national press juxtaposed with a major news story can be almost totally lost. With direct mail, dispatch can often be postponed until the moment at which it is most favourable. Although media advertising can be planned to react quickly to events, this can only occur in the national daily, or at best weekly, press. For many important business media, nearly six weeks must elapse between submission of the advertisement and publication. In the marketing of security, insurance, and financial services, where it may be important to be able to quickly point out accidents, failures, or disasters to audiences who might be subject to the same circumstances, direct mail can achieve an immediacy which is unobtainable through most other media.

Similarly, a too successful advertisement is likely to be an embarrassment, since most professional service companies cannot easily provide sufficient salesmen to deal on a personal level with inquiries which it stimulates. For example, a mailing covering 440 advertising agencies produced 33 replies in two days for a company selling design services. The design company held back the remainder of the mailing to enable it to clear the first inquiries. Had a press advertisement been used and achieved the same results, all the inquiries would have been received over a period of two or three days and the timelag before the last inquiry could be dealt with might well result in lost business.

For all these reasons, direct mail can be one of the most economic methods of promotion, but for other reasons it can be one of the most extravagant. Because of the control over the target audience and timing, economy can be ensured, but if the message itself is unremarkable the mailing will be totally wasted. The mail shot is unlikely to go further than the postroom wastepaper basket. Every businessman has a plethora of direct mail of one sort or another, some on such a regular basis that it is possible to discard many of them without opening since the label or envelope is recognizable; one professional association, in which the provision of management courses and books is an important activity, is renowned for its massive mailings which are certainly a source of irritation to many recipients. Similarly, conference sponsors also adopt the massive coverage approach, depending on a low rate of response from a high number of prospects. An advertising philosophy maintains that at any moment in time there are a finite number of firms considering the adoption of particular services. If a mail shot arrives at that moment, it will stimulate a reply. For all others, it will be wasted as a direct sales effort, but might contribute to longer-term selling. If this is so, it justifies the expense of massive coverage, and clearly it must be profitable for some companies to do this since they persist in their particular approach. However, for most companies, a policy of ensuring penetration to the right person at perhaps a higher cost per piece mailed is generally the best one.

This means that the contents themselves must be highly attention-getting and of apparently sufficient importance to pass through the screening personnel of postroom, secretaries, assistants, and others. One of the most effective ways of doing this is to address the prospect by name and to personalize the message as far as possible.

The usual form of direct mail adopted by professional service firms is that of a letter setting out the services available combined with a brochure, but even this somewhat conservative approach is regarded by many firms as brash. Nevertheless, there is a strong case for the use of gimmicks which are not themselves incompatible with the image objectives. For advertising agencies, for example, gimmickry can contribute to an image for attention-getting creative capability. A classical successful direct mail campaign, which did not conflict with the sales image, was the dispatch of a fresh rose each month to secretaries of managers who were actual or potential users of an airline and as a reminder of the airline's services and their interest in the client. A wristwatch calendar sent month by month through the year, each time accompanied by news items on the service company's activities, is an example of a continuous mailing programme which in the end became important to the recipients as the calendar was habit-forming and was missed if not received. A light touch can be adopted for perfectly serious services. A regular mailing of wire puzzles to clients and prospective clients by a firm of ergonomic consultants emphasizing their problem-solving capabilities in relation to physical forms of objects proved to be highly effective in terms of response and recall.

The essential thing about the use of gimmicks, it is emphasized, is to ensure their compatibility with the image of the service company and the service 'product'. Thus, combined with the advertising novelties referred to later in merchandising techniques, direct mail can be highly effective in terms of responses and as a contribution to total image build-up.

Direct mail gives the service firm more opportunity to explain its 'product' than press advertising. While economy in words and pictures is always necessary, it does not have to be applied so stringently as in press advertising. Moreover, it is possible to separate physically the elements of the direct mail mix, message, offer, and accompanying material, such as a giveaway, reply envelope, or cards.

If the effectiveness of mail shots is to be assessed, it will always be necessary to return to first principles and to know clearly what the direct mail campaign was intended to achieve. The importance of clear-cut promotional goals can never be overemphasized.

Thus, if the objective of the mail shot is to persuade recipients to send for further details, its effectiveness should not be measured in terms of business achieved, but in terms of responses for more information. Similarly, if the mailing is to open the way for personal selling, the measure of its success is not requests for more information by mail (however useful this may be), but the number of appointments the salesman obtains from recipients. However, even with such narrow goals, it is still not possible to make a totally accurate assessment of target achievements, since many elements other than the mailing may contribute to the action being measured. For example, a service company may be known to have successfully completed an assignment similar to one under consideration, but this information came from the press, not a mail shot. Under these circumstances, the attribution of an assignment to a direct mail campaign would only be partly accurate. However, even if total accuracy cannot be achieved a measure of relative success is still more than worth while, since it gives at least some criteria for comparison of effectiveness of different elements in the marketing and communications mix.

In the final analysis, attention-getting is not the ultimate measure of success of a direct mail campaign. It must also produce business. The attention-getting item, whether it is the message, a giveaway, or an invitation to reply for whatever incentive may be involved, is only a first step. The substance of the mailing or the follow-up must be attractive to the prospective buyer of the services either at the moment of reading, or seen to be of value for some later time and filed for reference or remembered.

Merchandising

The suggestion of merchandising in professional service marketing is perhaps the final heresy. If it is still very early to consider at all the marketing of professional services, then clearly merchandising is the one function of marketing that is least likely to be invoked. Slowly and surely other functions are being introduced—marketing research, advertising, public relations—to support what is the now, and by professional service standards at least, almost traditional, personal selling. It is possible that in future the success of professional service companies may depend as much on merchandising techniques as on any other single function.

There are probably as many definitions of merchandising as there are of marketing; indeed some of them will fit either activity equally well. They have in common, however, the understanding that all merchandising is concerned with activities at the point of sale.

Nothing could appear less appropriate than 'point of sale' in marketing professional services. Nevertheless, there is a 'point of sale' for all professional services as much as for any product. The fact that at the point of sale there is usually a salesman is neither here nor there.

Some services lend themselves more easily to merchandising devices than others. Banking, insurance, architecture, design consultancy, advertising, publishing, can all provide examples of adequate and effective merchandising

NAME	TECHNIQUE	EXAMPLES
Joint offer	'Package deal' where several services are needed to create a 'package' for the buyer	Banking, insurance, advertising, design consultancy, security
Trial offer	Test of a service with a 'no commitment' break clause	Security, estate management, employment agencies, factoring, stock audits
Gifts (advertising specialities)	Practical material such as sample size calculators, wristwatch calendars, slide-rules	All service companies
After-sales	Low cost monitoring, up-dating or maintenance service for the original assignment, creating regular contacts	Economic research, management consultancy, financial advice, location engineering, information retrieval
Shared cost	Multi-client projects, central subject with optional tailor-made extensions	Security, advertising, public relations, marketing and economic research
Client staff training	Instruction of staff to handle on-going activities after end of assignment	Debt control and collection, information retrieval, economic and marketing research, contract R & D, management consultancy, corporate planning
Point of sale literature	Brochures, displays, demonstration rooms, signs	Banking, insurance, estate management, surveying, architecture, trade and research associations
Special events	New premises, link with environmental factors, 'birthdays', unveiling of new technique	All service companies
Competitions	Awards usually given for a specific achievement in a given field, often associated with the service being promoted	All service companies (e.g., the Association of European Management Publishers' £4000 prize for the best management book)
Sponsored book	Book contributed or attributed to a member of a firm on a subject close to a firm's activities, examples taken from the firm's work but no other promotion; published by established publisher and sold through bookseller channels and distributed free or at reduced cost to potential client	Advertising agencies, management consultants, professional associations, engineering consultancy and contracting, architecture, medicine, law

Figure 11.5.

NAME	TECHNIQUE	EXAMPLES
Packaging	Attractive bindings for quotations and reports, novel forms of literature presentations and sales aids	All service companies
Sponsored event	Financial and/or promotional backing for an event related or not to the firm's activities	Banking, insurance, architecture (Barclays Bank 'four-in-hand carriage' event at Windsor Horse Show; *Financial Times* National Business Game)
Club sponsorship	Creating 'club' (more usually an association) for liaison and communication between practitioner and user	Exotic and new technique services: corporate long-range planning, Management by Objectives, planning programme budgeting systems (PPBS) (Industrial Advertising Association originally inspired and sponsored by a technical book publisher and a number of advertising agencies. Long Range Planning Society initiated by management consultancy firm)
Sponsored conference	Conference mounted to present information on a subject related to the service firm's expertise, usually with independent speakers as well as firm's speakers; paid attendance but with complimentary places for selected clients and potential clients	All service companies, but particularly contract R & D, insurance, security, executive search, engineering consultancy and contracting, mergers and amalgamations, (*Management of Research and Development* sponsored by Associated Business Programmes and Stanford Research Institute)
Academic sponsorship	Endowment of an institute, chair, research project, or sponsorship of a series of lectures	Services where the name is already sufficiently well known to enable the 'spin off' to register without additional promotion, but specifically banking, insurance, management consultancy (Hodge Chair of Banking & Accountancy at the University Institute, Cardiff, endowed by the Julian S. Hodge Group which provides financial services; Shell Chair of Chemical Engineering at Cambridge funded by Shell Petroleum)

Merchandising techniques for services

techniques. Management consultants, merger specialists, financial service companies, and others, have greater problems. Thus, the applicability of the major merchandising techniques needs individual consideration.

There are so many merchandising methods and devices that it would be futile to attempt to list them all, and in any event only a few are applicable to the merchandising of professional services. Moreover, those methods which are applicable require disguising to hide their consumer goods marketing antecedents if they are to be considered at all. Just how applicable merchandising techniques might be can be concluded from Figure 11.5 in which no attempt has been made to hide their origins.

Some are time-honoured methods used by even the most conservative of companies, even though not necessarily seen as direct promotional activity. The endowment of university chairs and sponsoring of research projects by industrial and commercial concerns are excellent examples. It could be argued that the endowment is to benefit the firm only in a technical sense. The point is a weak one: if this were the only purpose, why include the name of the company in the endowment?

The strong impression exists so far as the non-sponsored activities are concerned that, given more technical or less obviously consumer gimmick names, the techniques would be far more acceptable for professional service marketing. Referring to 'joint offer' as 'turnkey' may provide or encourage a view of the offer which is more compatible with the needs of both the service provider and his customer. 'Club appeal' presented as 'synergistic interface' and 'after sales' as 'project monitoring' may do nothing for communications, but a great deal to enhance the acceptability and respectability of a perfectly valid marketing method.

The effective use of any of the techniques described is not likely to occur unless their applicability to professional service companies can be seen. In this context 'applicability' must also include compatibility with the service company's perception of itself and its clients and, conversely, the clients' perception of the suppliers of services. Gaining an acceptance for promotional techniques among professional service companies will not be made easier by calling a spade a spade, that is expressing them in the more strident terms of consumer goods mass marketing. Nevertheless, whichever way they are disguised, the similarity between the two areas is manifest. Perhaps, therefore, there is a case, at least for the moment, for sophistry by cloaking the various terms in a more acceptable camouflage.

12

Pricing

> The Association of Consulting Engineers has reaffirmed the principle that members must not knowingly compete with each other on professional charges ... there had been recent difficulties after prospective clients had invited a number of consulting engineers to submit either priced proposals or budget estimates for professional services. That must not be done unless a member was assured that no other consulting engineer was being so invited, the Association said.[1]

While the effects of the Monopolies Commission on professional service pricing may outlaw such dictums as these, this one does illustrate the attitude of the professional associations and, it must be presumed, their members to indulging in price competition.

The *raison d'être* of the rules of practice promulgated and policed by many professions is to avoid price competition. Thus, discussion on price for many services would appear to be largely academic. Indeed, there is some truth in this because while price fixing has been roundly condemned and outlawed for almost all goods (books being an exception), charges for services continue 'standard' (which is a euphemism for 'fixed') in many professions; conveyancing charges by solicitors, property sales commissions by estate agents, scales of fees by architects and many types of insurance premiums, and for some bank services. Besides those prices which are enforceable legally or by professional associations, there is a whole structure of 'accepted' prices such as the major management consultants adopt for *per diem* charges, literary and advertising agencies for commission, and doctors for consultation.

Nevertheless, even within these restricted fields, there is room for more profitable operation by the use of pricing as a marketing tool or weapon, depending on how the service companies regard price. Outside the areas of

[1] *The Financial Times* (London, 3 July 1970).

fixed, standard, or customary prices, the use of pricing in the marketing mix remains primitive and awaits only intelligent application for substantial rewards to be reaped. Pricing strategy is nothing more than the art of projecting and directing the larger pricing issues within a marketing campaign in order to maximize profit over whatever term the corporate or marketing plans are required to cover.

There should be no confusion, however, between price strategies and price cutting; they are not the same thing. Indeed, a price strategy may demand the opposite to price cutting—price inflation. In every type of transaction, not just services, it is far better for competition not to be based on a selling price which is destructive to the seller and may be harmful to the buyer, as the national airlines, for example, appreciated many years ago. They recognized that price competition could lead to lowering of aircraft safety standards, not just cabin standards, and through their association developed a complex and comprehensive system of price maintenance which they justified on grounds of passenger safety. However, to say price cutting is usually destructive is not to imply that prices should not be flexible or be manipulated, since the use of pricing strategies, designed for specific situations and to achieve specified objectives, is an effective means of competition.

Costing and pricing
The use of pricing strategies in industrial goods generally lacks even the little sophistication that exists in the consumer goods field, while in services they are virtually non-existent. In part, this stems from the inadequacies of most costing methods for services which still operate by the 'faith, hope, and 50 per cent' method. The vagaries in costing and pricing the output of advertising agencies, consulting firms, and other professional service activities, have caused many of their managements to adopt empirical and *ad hoc* approaches. One result is that while management of professional service firms can determine the profitability of the enterprise as a whole, they cannot often calculate the profit or loss contribution of individual assignments, customers, or even services. This, in turn, means that the development of a pricing strategy is virtually useless because the target for the strategy cannot be accurately identified.

It has rightly been argued[1] that service company managements are not in full control of their operations unless they *do* develop a reliable system of 'product' or project cost accounting. Accountants and management consultants throw up their hands in horror when they find that their clients do not know with exactitude the cost of the products they are selling. Nevertheless, these and other professional service providers have either neglected or ignored this problem in relation to themselves, relying on the total profitability of their operations to ensure continuing activity. Once more the *sartor*

[1] H E McDonald and T L Stromberger, 'Cost Control for the Professional Firm', *Harvard Business Review* (Cambridge, Mass., January/February 1969).

resartus syndrome shows itself to the detriment of the image of the service providers.

This type of situation is as inefficient as it is unnecessary, since a professional service firm can and should be able to identify costs. The reasons for the neglect are numerous and require study as a first step to rectifying the position. McDonald and Stromberger[1] have suggested that the major difference between professional service and other firms is the product-cost characteristics.

- The 'product' made by the professional service firm is often difficult to describe and measure.
- Its costs are primarily 'people' costs—payroll, benefits, insurance, bonuses, deferred compensation, pensions, etc. These costs, they suggest, typically range between 70 per cent and 80 per cent of total operating costs and between 55 per cent and 70 per cent of gross income.
- The remaining operating costs—rent, travel, insurance, office supplies, etc.—are usually directly related to the level of people costs.
- People are more difficult to cost than machines. A machine may be on or off, and normally runs a fixed number of hours with a given output. This is not so with people. 'People' output can be increased for a time, at least, with little or no additional gross costs.

The relevance of these characteristics within the context of pricing is simply that no price level can be fixed or manipulation of price take place successfully unless the cost of the service is known—thus the development of a price strategy which is meaningful is out of the question without a basic knowledge of the nature of costs.

Strategies for successful pricing

The moment, however, the service company looks at the techniques which enable it to devise and operate a pricing strategy, it finds itself faced with a dichotomy. These are the approaches offered by price theorists engaged in developing a simplified model that helps to understand complicated reality and the approaches of marketing specialists discussing pricing on a descriptive level explaining what businessmen do, or say they do. Neither procedure is satisfactory. The model is limited in use by psychological aspects of pricing—that is the psychology of seller as well as buyer—and the empiric approach quickly reveals a lack of vital information. Either concepts or practices alone are insufficient and probably misleading. A combination and balance is needed, but difficult to achieve. This situation should be recognized in considering the strategies suggested.

Fortunately, writers on pricing have been more sensitive to the needs of service businesses than most other authors working in the marketing field,

[1] Ibid.

so that the service provider does not find himself having to translate from tangible to intangible terms.

Developing pricing strategies is an exercise which must be undertaken on two dimensions. First, it is necessary to think in terms of establishing the right price and, second, of using the correct methodology to arrive at it. The latter is perhaps an even more crucial exercise in a service business than in most other enterprises. Correct pricing for service companies is perhaps more important than for product companies because of the economic structure of the service business. Employing as they do relatively little capital implies that pricing and time utilization are the primary elements of leverage in achieving profitability. Moreover, as many service businesses are less subject to the pressures and controls of the market place than manufacturing businesses, they can adopt greater flexibility in pricing. The professional service company, for most of the time, is in the 'value sensitive' not 'price sensitive' area shown in Figure 6.3, page 58.

In order to establish the alternatives available from which the mix can be derived, six basic methods of pricing have been identified[1] and explained and can be advantageously followed.

1 Cost pricing: a conventional method of arriving at price by summating the chargeable cost. Price is arrived at for various levels of activity and time utilization which will yield the desired profit. This method is generally only used in service businesses for their non-professional activities.

2 Competitive pay pricing: a variation of the cost-pricing system based on the average or competitive salary levels for the professionals involved and charged for the time utilized. Typically this approach is used for government work where the time rates are virtually set by the buyer. This method means that price is determined by cost, and cost for the service firm is largely determined by payroll, not materials, machinery, or stocks.

3 Contingency payment pricing: this is essentially the service equivalent of piecework rates in manufacturing or commission for salesmen. The fee for services performed is contingent upon a certain act being performed or by accomplishment. The method is used by executive search companies and employment agencies, in brokerage deals, estate management, and other services.

4 Fixed price: a uniformity achieved by a controlling body. This may be government (fees payable to dentists for national health service treatment), professional associations (solicitors' conveyancing fees), or informal agreements (*per diem* for management consultants). Fixed pricing, as Sibson points out,[2] is the result of a pricing decision, not a method of reaching it, although it might have been arrived at using one of the other methods described.

[1] R E Sibson, 'A Service', *Creative Pricing*, E Marting, ed. American Management Association (New York, 1968). Pp. 147–152.
[2] Ibid, P. 150.

5 Contract pricing: this is a method of fixed pricing, but not by agreement so much as by contract. For example, rebates for insurance services such as reimbursable provisions in contracts covering group insurance. One effect of contract pricing is the removal of pricing from the competitive mix since the offer price is fixed, often by the buyer.
6 Value pricing: or what the market will bear. Other methods are only rough guides to value. Value pricing assumes that buyers will respond to price in accordance with the value they place on the service. This is common practice in public seminar sponsoring and economic and social research.

Alfred Oxenfeldt suggests another approach which, while involving some of the foregoing, has the inestimable advantage of taking into account both financial and psychological factors.[1] Oxenfeldt suggests as the main groups for consideration the following:

- considerations involving members of the firm;
- considerations involving customers;
- considerations involving competitors;
- considerations involving resellers (only occasionally applicable to services);
- considerations involving suppliers;
- considerations involving government;
- considerations involving new products;
- considerations involving market conditions.

Both the Sibson and Oxenfeldt studies justify close examination by professional service companies faced with the creation of pricing strategies.

Pricing tactics
The strategy, however it is devised, must lead towards the determination of the shorter-term tactical considerations and, in its final form, designate the actual price to be charged.

In terms of tactical consideration, the same semantic problem as with merchandising occurs. The pricing techniques used in consumer goods marketing adequately describe some of the range of possibilities open to professional service firms, but they tend to be rejected because of their connotation and, as with merchandising, this is quite wrong. With modifications to allow for the intangibility of the 'product' they can be applied effectively and profitably. A number of major tactics are listed in Figure 12.1.

Examples of the use of each type of pricing tactic are to be seen throughout the service industries. Loss leading is frequently practised in PR, design consultancy, marketing consultancy, and translation services, and is not unknown in accountancy or the legal profession. Offset pricing can be found

[1] A R Oxenfeldt, *Pricing for Marketing Executives*. Wadsworth (Belmont, Calif., 1966). Pp. 77–85.

NAME	DESCRIPTION	EFFECT
'Loss leader'	Deliberately deflated price to obtain 'first' business or to 'get in'	Successful with unsophisticated buyers, but tends to give a price ceiling which is difficult to penetrate later
'Offset'	Low basic price with recouping on extra 'services' or time, e.g., project costed on time basis with extras computed at end of project	Psychologically favourable at the tendering stage, but can easily lead to difficulties on implementation. Advantages in some cases of client being able to control extent of commitment
'Diversionary'	Low basic price on selected services to develop image of low cost structure which 'rubs off' on total operation	Generally effective so long as no suggestion of 'switch selling' is allowed to develop
'Discrete'	Price pitched to bring a decision into the area of authority of a DMU favouring the service company. A lower price may take decision to lower management; a high price to the board. This tactic necessarily requires an intimate knowledge of the prospect firm	While the decision can be moved into the DMU responsibility area favouring the service or better able to appreciate the offer, price movements upwards or downwards have associated risks
'Discount'	Price quotation subject to discounts on a predetermined basis, e.g., time schedule, extent of commitment, magnitude of projects	Positive encouragement to buyer to structure project on mutually favourable basis. Danger that assignment objectives may get distorted
'Guarantee'	Price includes an undertaking to achieve certain results—the guarantee out-guaranteeing competitors	Moves competition from prices to value area and places high-quality service in most favourable posture to compete with low quality service
'Price lining'	Price kept constant but quality or extent of service adjusted to reflect changes in costs	Removes price as major negotiating point, substituting the service 'product', but note effect above for 'diversionary' pricing

Figure 12.1 Pricing tactics

in advertising, where a large number of 'extras' can be added to basic costs or in addition to the commission received from the media owners.

Diversionary pricing is a phenomenon encountered in various types of consultancy, educational services, and in some types of agency services, such as those offered by literary and theatrical agents. Prior to the 'unbundling' which the US government imposed on their computer industry, it was possible to find an element of both offset and diversionary pricing in the marketing tactics which forced buyers of hardware to purchase programmes also. Discrete pricing can be found in use by all professional service firms not bound by price regulations, and where the knowledge of the buying processes and DMU is high. Discount pricing is known in information services, computer bureaux, leasing, and security services. Guarantee pricing is practised, albeit sometimes unconsciously, in engineering consultancy, but also in professional services where price control is exercised. Price lining is not unknown in educational services, some types of panel market research, insurance and property management, and consultancy services based on a 'job cost' not *per diem*.

Precisely how each tactic is used is totally dependent upon the service involved, the target client group, and what might be termed the 'ambient conditions'. Whatever the circumstances, the use of any of these tactics, to be effective, requires a knowledge and understanding of the market and the buying process.

Any talk of pricing in professional services is surrounded with a type of taboo typified at its extreme by the barrister who receives not a fee but an honorarium, and all financial arrangements are negotiated through his clerk. (Barristers, by the way, still carry on their gowns the vestigial remains of the pocket into which the fee was placed to avoid them actually having to receive the money from the instructing solicitor.) Thus, pricing tactics are frequently seen, not as they are—a legitimate and efficient tool of marketing—but as a somewhat devious means of separating the client from his money. Nothing could be further from the truth. Just as in merchandising, if the nomenclatures and connotations of pricing tactics create a semantic blockage to their utilisation, then there is a case for changing the titles. However, whether you call it a 'loss leader', 'development pricing', or a 'sprat to catch a mackerel', the tactic remains the same and is wholly applicable to professional service marketing.

Deciding the price

When the strategy has been decided and the tactics to be used agreed, there still remains the basic problem of arriving at the actual price to be charged. The multistage approach to pricing provides a concise and very practical guide for arriving at the offer price:[1] it begins with the identification of the

[1] A R Oxenfeldt, 'Multi-Stage Approach to Pricing', *Harvard Business Review* (Cambridge' Mass., July/August 1960).

market targets (segmentation); it then considers the selection and development of an appropriate image (psychological factors); moves on to designating the marketing mix which will reinforce the image and achieve the sales commensurate with the planned level of output; next, the pricing policy is determined (e.g., the extent of price flexibility—matching with 'average' or competitors); choice of price strategy—long-term considerations ignoring random movements and events; finally, selection of the specific price within the parameters which have been defined by the preceding steps.

Oxenfeldt's multistage approach differs from the usual method of arriving at a price in two major respects. It demands a long-range view of price by emphasizing the enduring effects of most price actions on a company and its service image, and it allows the price decision to be made in stages rather than demanding a simultaneous solution of the entire problem.

One further point requires comment. For many types of professional services, the method of quotation is by bidding, and thus price setting takes place under circumstances of imperfect competition in that knowledge of the market is far from complete—who is competing, the nature of the offer, and, of course, price. Competitive bidding may be the cornerstone of the free enterprise system and work well for products, but it is monumentally inefficient in terms of service purchasing, if only because of the three factors which professional services and marketing must take cognizance: reducing uncertainty, understanding problems, and demonstrating professionalism. Purchasing professional services tends to make the buyer treat service firms as 'suppliers', which leads the buyer naturally to attempt to secure bids for what they consider essentially 'equivalent' offerings, or at least offerings whose differences can be readily identified and evaluated. The response to tenders may be identical, but the approaches will tend to vary widely for professional services and are not in the true sense comparable.

However, since the system is prevalent, it is as well to consider how it might best be manipulated. Competitive bidding, it has been pointed out,[1] is an art as well as a science. There are many non-quantifiable variables such as competitors' attitudes towards a contract, strategies which are based more on preventing a particular firm from getting the contract than on the bidder's desire to obtain it for himself, or the individual firms' and competitors' need for the contract. A close approximation of such variables as these must be considered an art. Any system devised to maximize chances of success by tendering firms in competitive bidding in order to succeed must nevertheless integrate these variables with the quantifiable factors, particularly labour, out-of-pocket expenses, and marketing costs.

The technique developed in industries, where competitive bidding is endemic or standard routine, usually depends on historical knowledge of successful bid prices in order to arrive at a range of prices for future bi

[1] L B Bell, 'A System of Competitive Bidding', *Journal of Systems Management* (Cleveland, Ohio, March 1969).

This information is frequently available in the public sector and among some other purchasing groups, but it is not always obtainable in professional service markets. This is partly because the professional service marketer very often feels that it is neither tactful nor in keeping with his image of himself to discuss competitive pricing and thereby (to him) reduce the whole process to the level of a Levantine market-place.

Successful competitive bidding, like any form of pricing, requires good historical information bases. Ideally, the pricing strategy in a competitive bid should be based on:

- estimate of direct cost;
- amount of past bids which were successful (where relevant);
- average of all bids received;
- identification of the bidders;
- amount of each individual bid;
- each bid as percentage of own direct cost estimate;
- estimate of each bidder's workload.

By developing a dossier on each competitor, given that most of the information is available and allowing that some may be subjective, it is possible to narrow the price band in which any individual quotation may be made. It may have proved possible to develop a correlation between prices and some of the factors listed. Because so many professional services have standard or accepted cost rates (usually on a per day basis), the effort of building up cost data is made simpler. However, the problem of the allocation of indirect costs is no less for the service firm than for the manufacturer.

The creation of a model of the bid situation provides considerable guidance in deciding the bid price. This model comprises the mathematical relationships which describe to a sufficient degree of approximation the behaviour of the physical system—company, competition, customer. The function of the model is nothing more than the evaluation and interpretation of the inputs and their interactions. In basic terms, the model will provide a rational evaluation of the potential profit resulting from the acquisition of the contract and the potential loss resulting from failure to obtain it. The evaluation is made against the background of uncertainty caused by imperfect knowledge of the customers' and competitors' behaviour. The model permits payoff to be evaluated against risk, while recognizing that the achievement of the payoff is subject to uncertainty. The size of the payoff and the expectation of obtaining it are both dependent on the bid price, while the size of the risk is quite independent of the bid price.

A high price will lead to a substantial profit, but a low chance of success; a low price might ensure success, but could result in low profit or no profit. Thus, both ends of the scale lead to a low profit expectation, but for different reasons. Somewhere within this range there is a price which represents the optimum trade-off between profitability and success probability.

In arriving at this price, analysis is needed to show:

- marginal profit contribution of the contract;
- marginal loss penalty incurred if contract is lost;
- probability of success at any given price and within a specified environment.

This analysis will enable the bid price to be determined which will maximize the profit expectation from the contract, with profit expectation considered equal to marginal profit contribution times success probability less the product of marginal loss penalty times failure probability ($PE = MPC \times SP - MLP \times FP$).

This approach has been applied and tested many times for product tendering and is applicable to professional service bids. A full description of the methodology with a most useful and detailed case study of its use has been prepared.[1]

While the approaches which have been briefly outlined are well worth further study, they do not solve the problems of pricing in a competitive bid situation. However, they make the assessments which are so necessary in these situations that much easier to apply. No amount of scientific analysis will replace these judgements, because the bid price in the end is the result of weighing up both the independent judgements and the quantifiable factors and making yet another judgement on the implications of the balance struck in terms of the price it is finally decided to quote.

The problem and rewards of effective pricing techniques as part of the marketing mix have been treated only superficially in this chapter—more as an introduction to a subject rarely considered by professional service marketers than as a description of its mechanics. The purpose is to bring pricing within the consideration of professional service firms or to induce a re-examination of traditional pricing concepts.

At one extreme, price will be the key decision factor, such as in the purchase of non-differentiated products and services, and, at the other extreme, it will be of no consequence within the restraints imposed by the buyer's resources, for example, medical advice in an emergency. Between these limits price will play a variable role in the range of factors considered in deciding both on the use of a service and on the provider of that service. Reference to Figure 6.3, page 58, shows that the greater the innovation the further into the value sensitive area the decision is moved, and the less is the importance of price. This does not mean, however, that price can be arrived at in an arbitrary manner ignoring internal and external factors. Price setting at the correct level is of considerable consequence both for the individual decision and for the survival of the company.

[1] F Edelman, 'Art and Science of Competitive Bidding', *Harvard Business Review* Cambridge, Mass., July/August 1965).

Price is a weapon, or a tool, to obtain business as well as to ensure the profitable continuance of the firm. The two objectives are interrelated and lend themselves to a variety of strategies for their successful achievement. The marketer of professional services, faced with increasing professionalism in marketing, needs an understanding of pricing if he is to have any chance of success.

13

Service strategy

> A peculiar characteristic of the accountancy profession has been its policy of preoccupation with the present to the detriment of the future. Little emphasis has been placed upon the need to explore and define the multiplicity of uses to which accounting can be put. Only in isolated instances has the question ever been asked, for what uses—other than traditional ones—can the professional skill of accountants be utilized?[1]

These words, written nearly 20 years ago, accurately reflect an attitude still prevalent in large parts of this profession and many others, and it is one which blocks off the development of new services from consideration, let alone action.

Yet a vital part of any marketing activity is, of course, product development. The intangibility of services does not in any way reduce the need for planned development of the services offered, and, indeed, in this context the service is often referred to as the 'product'. For example, travel agencies, travel wholesalers, and tourist boards always refer to the 'holiday product'.

As will be obvious from the description of the strategy components in chapter 9, 'Market Strategy and Planning', the selection of the service 'product' and the development of the service mix represent major strategic decisions which will determine almost all else that will be done within the company, whether it be manpower planning, motivation, or the marketing mix.

An important consideration, and, indeed, often the initial mistake of the professional service firm adopting the marketing concept, is to restrict its perspectives and to limit its consideration of market opportunities by taking the existing service 'product' as the basic target in planning marketing activities. If, however, the service 'product' is seen as a means of reaching the sales

[1] Nicholas A H Stacey, *English Accountancy 1800–1954*. Gee (London, 1954). P. xii.

targets, the need for analysis of 'product' alternatives and the constant search for new 'product' ideas is highlighted.

Because most service companies originate on the basis of the skills of their initiators, and because these skills are all too often seen too narrowly by them, the question of 'product' development is usually neglected. The dangers of too parochial a view of a business were never better highlighted than by Theodore Levitt,[1] and as it happens some of his oft-quoted examples are from the service industries.

'Product' policy has two dimensions. First, the decisions which govern the inclusion of services within the total range offered by the firm and, second, the search for new services to add to the existing range or to replace existing services.

Service mix

The pressure for a greater variety of services comes from both the service firm seeking to exploit under-utilized resources and growth, and from the client looking for variations from the standard services which will better fit his total requirements, whether they are commercial or technical.

Thus, professional service firms are faced with the need for, and the opportunity to offer, not a single service but a range of services—insurance companies not just life insurance, but also accident, marine, fire; merchant banks not just the provision of finance but investment management, foreign exchange, letters of credit and collections, and public issues; management consultants not just organization studies and restructuring, but education, operational research, and production engineering. For most companies, sales tend to be concentrated over a few of the available services. The 80:20 rule applies: that is, 80 per cent of sales are transacted over 20 per cent of the services offered. No formula has yet been devised for finding out under what circumstances a firm can be more profitable by either increasing or narrowing its width of services and the depth in which they are offered.[2] The decision as to the correct mix is a difficult one. How extensive should the range of services be and what effect will a wide range have on the image of the service company? What is the spread of demand likely to be over the entire range? What is the optimum-minimum range?

So far, only an empirical approach can provide indications of the answers to these questions, and it is usually impossible to assess what would have happened had the opposite decision been taken. The essential nature of the problem is to determine what role each service in the mix plays, even if it is only a poor performer. For example, in order to be seen by clients to be

[1] *Innovation in Marketing.* Pan Books (London, 1968). Chapter 3.
[2] Range *width* can be defined as a number of different options of services of the same genre, for example: market research, advertising research, image research. Range *depth* would be alternatives available within any one type, for example: advertising research into media, attitudes, perceptions, recall.

seriously in a business, the service firm may have to offer a bigger 'package' than the viability of individual elements of the 'package' may justify. Nevertheless, the image impact of the full line is frequently an important decision-making factor which will improve the competitive position of one firm against another. Management trained in accountancy rather than marketing disciplines find this concept difficult to understand, since the return on a single service may not appear to justify its presence in the range yet its contribution to the marketability of other services may be considerable.

One of the major uses of industrial marketing research is to determine the needs of users and potential users of professional services in terms of the type, quality, and extent of services required. Research in this context, however, is not merely to quantify a likely demand and to probe any synergy or negative synergy which will occur in the adoption of an additional service. A more important task is to examine the image aspects and implications of the extended or adjusted range. Will the additional or changed service make the service company more credible in its existing or potential markets? Will it produce the opposite effect on a firm desperately in search of its true role? Will the existence of a variation in the basic service range, while not itself generating turnover, add to the attractiveness of other services? For example, the addition of a PR department in an advertising agency, even if it is not a profitable adjunct in itself, can produce a greater feeling of security among advertising agency clients. They may well feel that if PR was needed in their promotional mix, the agency, having its own in-house facilities, would not seek to avoid undertaking this work. Thus, they would be buying more objective advice. Professional firms operating internationally may do so with complete efficiency and competence working from their home base, yet in many fields the lack of overseas offices or associates makes a company less than credible. Thus, organizations often build a network of associates or correspondents, knowing full well that the network is largely 'window dressing.' The network is required to establish credibility. However, once established, it can be used for a number of other purposes—license research, capacity search, market monitoring, barter deals, government liaison, on-the-spot help for visitors. The service firm can spin off an expanded range of services which require the international coverage image.

Thus, the basic sources of information on which range decisions can be made are from the clients or would-be clients themselves, from internal factors, and also from the competitive environment. The actions necessary to work outward from these three sources, but not necessarily in the order given, are:

- identification of market targets;
- study of lost business to determine how far it is attributable to lack of a required service or apparent lack of capability in the service area concerned;

- quantification of existing service 'packages' and relating them to client needs;
- research into client buying needs (what do our clients buy from others they could buy from us?);
- study of internal capabilities for range extension;
- study of competitive offerings;
- examination of changes in content or coverage of existing services which would provide a new or improved facility for clients.

In consumer goods markets, there are many notable examples of successful product range strategies as widely different as those adopted by Fortnum & Mason and Marks & Spencer. Each is correct for the market segment being serviced. In the mass-produced sector of the consumer goods industry, the process of range development has been brought to a fine art (but not a science) by the breaking down of the buying process into selection, procurement, and merchandising. In industrial goods the lack of any soundly based theory of range optimization and the almost totally empiric nature of the practice of developing ranges bedevils all aspects of product strategy, whether it is for raw materials, capital goods, operating supplies, or services. There seems little sign that the marketing theorists are going to be able to provide marketers of goods or services with a formula for optimum range development in the foreseeable future. Trial and error used with a wide information base will at least give reliable guidelines until a more scientific method can be adopted.

Developing new services[1]
The second dimension of product policy to be considered is the development of new services to add to the existing range or to replace those which have 'topped out'.[2]

In considering new services, there is a danger in treating them in isolation from the existing services, and although this division is made here for the sake of clarity it is not a realistic one. Many of the techniques and approaches suggested for optimizing ranges by extensions and changes in the basic 'product' groups are also relevant for new 'product' development. Figure 13.1 illustrates the four possible courses of action firms usually consider.

Situations 1 and 2 may involve changing the 'product' mix. Situations 3 and 4 call for new products.

However, just where the new services and ideas on which they are based are to come from is usually far from clear. There are, of course, within every company, 'stables' of ideas awaiting a winner to be drawn from them: there are personnel with their own particular propositions and there are formal, but usually unstructured, attempts to feed through new ideas either via the

[1] 'New' in this context refers to new for the company and not necessarily new in the innovative sense.
[2] The term 'top out' refers to the position on the life cycle curve at which a continuous decline in sales occurs until the service is finally withdrawn as no longer viable and has thus ended its life cycle.

SITUATION	RESOURCE
1 Attempting to sell more existing services to existing clients	Existing capability, facilities, and market position
2 Attempting to sell existing services to new clients	Existing capabilities and facilities. No market resources
3 Attempting to sell new services to existing clients	Market resources, no existing capability or facility resource
4 Attempting to sell new services in new markets	Nil

Figure 13.1. New service options

suggestion box equivalent in the service firm, by brainstorming, or by waiting for that most ephemeral of all qualities, inspiration.

This *mélange* of idea generation is quite the most usual, even in companies which sell as their expertise 'creativity'. The creative problem-solver, irrespective of his area of expertise, is often incapable of being *consistently* creative on his own behalf. This perhaps accounts for the persistently high rate of failure among service companies and a generally low level of profitability.[1]

To begin with, it is necessary to draw the definition for what comprises a 'new service' as widely as possible. A highly practical and useful grouping which avoids the hazard of an artificial dichotomy between new and old, and which links to the situation/resource situation in Figure 13.1, has been developed.[2]

● Second and subsequent generation services.
● 'Products' new to the service firm's range and mix, but in basic functional form already available on the market serviced.
● Services already available, but adapted for a new market.
● Totally new services.

Once the definition of what constitutes a new product has been formulated, consideration of the ways in which each type may evolve has value in that it enables the boundaries of searching to be set. 'Open mind' searching, lacking a focal point or confines, risks waste in the examination of search areas which have no relevance.[3]

Resource-based services
A study of resources should be the first task of the service firm seeking to adjust the range of services it offers. The techniques already described in

[1] For example, while financial and professional service firms comprised 0.03 per cent of all business establishments in 1969, they accounted for 3.7 per cent of all receiving orders under Section 130 of the Bankruptcy Act, 1914.
[2] Mary Griffin, 'Generation of New Product Ideas', *The Marketing of Industrial Products*. Aubrey Wilson, ed. Pan Books (London, 1972). P. 24.
[3] Ibid.

chapter 8, 'Identifying Market Opportunities', plus the identification of what can be developed as a USP (Unique Selling Proposition), provides the first step. The danger already referred to, however, of treating the 'product' as the objective of the exercise, rather than the satisfaction of a real market need, must be avoided. The use of all the skills and apparatus of marketing to lure the customer to the 'product' is a negation of the marketing concept.

It is truly surprising how rarely well organized and managed firms have failed to audit all the areas in which they have capability. This is because of the intangibility of this capability. Whereas it is common practice to maintain detailed inventories of equipment, managers of firms selling human skills will frequently not know that their personnel have capabilities beyond those for which they were specifically employed. For instance, a statistician in a transport economics consultancy group was found to be an expert in Latin-American trade only when he published a major study on the area, and this is a typical example of the possession of capabilities which are neither documented nor utilized. Clearly, a listing of capabilities and resources can, for many companies, be the first important step towards developing range variables of the type which will more fully exploit their resources.

Studying the opportunities from the customer end of the spectrum calls into use industrial marketing research which can be employed to determine the requirements of actual and potential clients, both fulfilled and, more importantly, unfulfilled. However, it is in the interpretation of these needs that the major skills are required because, while the marketer must appraise and attempt to meet the buyer's requirements, any course of action which is detrimental to the service supplying firm cannot be justified. The firm that is at the mercy of its customers deserves sympathy and nothing else. Thus, a balance is required between the demands of the user of services and that which it is profitable for the service company to supply.

Ideally, the resources available or acquirable should be matched with the services the user wishes to purchase and offered under the conditions which make them acceptable.

This two-dimensional study will provide an important input of service possibilities which, combined with a study of the competitive climate, not just directly competitive but also indirectly competitive, will define services for consideration. These can then be screened by the normal product selection process[1] and developed in terms of their market acceptability and internal compatibility with corporate resources and aspirations.

New services from old

New services can often evolve from client requests for higher performance standards or new additional features for an old service. The professional association concerned with R & D may well find their membership has a

---

[1] A screening process for products which is adaptable for services is set out in detail in: Aubrey Wilson, *The Art and Practice of Marketing*. Hutchinson (London, 1971). Pp. 60–74.

requirement for management consultancy. This was the experience of the Production Engineering Research Association which established such a facility for members. Similarly, under the influence of demand from customers, banking has added in the last few years many more services to its total offering, including such completely new facilities as credit cards.

New service ideas will, of course, also derive from changes within the client company and the environment. For example, the use of new materials, components, or techniques, or a change in manufacturing process, can invoke the need for computer software consultancy; a new physical product may demand the services of a systems engineer; increasing demand on the client's support services could produce a requirement for a location engineering study. All these might well be grafted on the existing 'product' range of a variety of professional service firms already supplying other services to these types of companies.

Many management services are designed to, and succeed in, solving a company's problems, but do not leave clients with a capability which enables them to solve their own problems on future occasions. Thus, a demand for many types of management services may, in turn, lead to a demand that they should be so structured as to include personnel training which will permit the firm to handle similar problems in the future without recourse to outside assistance.

Yet another area is human engineering. Increased industrial unrest stemming from decreasing levels of job satisfaction may well offer opportunities for the PR company, executive search and employment agencies, and consulting engineers to move into the field of industrial sociology and psychology.

The three principles of application engineering, value analysis, and human engineering, combined together, form the systems engineering approach which, at its simplest, is the creation of a new service by the technical and commercial study of processes, methods, and other systems, to determine whether a new service or a new combination of existing services cannot improve the activity to which they are to be applied. The systems approach differs only from the other approaches in that it is an interdisciplinary and an orderly, not a random 'architectural', approach for dealing with complex problems of choice under conditions of uncertainty. The task of the analyst is to specify a closed operating network in which the components will work together so as to yield the optimum balance of economy, efficiency, and risk minimization.

The approach is applied in what is a normal scientific sequence of events. The following has been suggested:[1]

- definition of the problem;
- testing the definition;
- building a model;

[1] Lee Adler, 'Systems Approach to Marketing', *Harvard Business Review* (Cambridge, Mass., May/June 1967).

- setting concrete objectives;
- developing alternative solutions;
- deciding criteria for tests of relative value;
- quantification of some or all of the factors or variables;
- manipulation of the model;
- verification of results.

The systems approach to marketing professional services, and particularly new service development from old services, is a methodical operation within a frame of reference which includes all aspects of the problem to be considered. It enables the coordinated deployment of all appropriate tools of marketing to occur. Greater efficiency and economy can be achieved and the quicker recognition of impending problems is made possible by better understanding of the complex interplay of many trends and forces to be perceived. Finally, it is a stimulant to innovation and a means of quantitatively verifying results.[1]

New services for present markets
This approach, like the previous one, depends for its success on an understanding of the operations and requirements of clients and potential clients and constant monitoring of these needs: these studies almost invariably produce, as a spin off, information needs on peripheral markets.

The approach termed 'industries we serve' simply asks: 'What services do our clients buy which they do not buy from us but which we could provide?' It is basically an exploitation of market resources rather than 'production' resources. The approach may involve a much higher degree of diversification in comparison to the substantially linear mode of expansion so far discussed. New technical skills and, possibly, physical resources may be needed as well as a new 'image' and substance for capability in the chosen field.

Most architects practising up to about 1945 confined their services to construction projects. Since then, many firms have extended their range of services in one direction to include planning in all its aspects, and in another to electrical and mechanical engineering. Architects' clients buy far more services than architects traditionally supplied, hence the development of more complete 'packages'.

Perhaps no better or more successful example of developing a new service for existing markets has occurred than in some parts of the accountancy profession. The leading companies were in an unusually good vantage position to observe the problems of their clients. By grafting a management consultancy arm on to their business, some accounting companies were able to offer a totally new service in clearly identified areas of need, starting from a point of total credibility and a position in buying process terms of 'sitting tenants'.

[1] Ibid.

The problem of defining search areas of the kind envisaged here is essentially similar to that of designing a faceted system for the classification of information. The aim is the fullest exploitation of all the skills and resources associated with the service or a service mix, whether these are technical or commercial. Each must therefore be considered in turn by isolating the generic heading under which it falls and then investigating the potential offered by others coming within the same category.

Old services for new markets

Existing services can always be considered for new markets, since in these markets they may represent a new service. The possibilities of technological transfer are as great for services as for products. Industrial marketing research came about from the application of consumer research techniques in non-consumer markets, and it is claimed that consumer research itself was evolved from operational research conducted in industry. The 'one stop' financial services concept now taking off in the United States is the application of the techniques of one type of service into new areas of financial operations.

It is also true that services which have 'topped out' in one industry may be an innovation in another. The time lag of the acceptance of a service across industry can be a span of years. Similarly, the application of professional services in less well-developed overseas areas may also offer new opportunities.

Searches for new markets for services entail envisaging all the possible applications of a service, the techniques embodied in it, or those employed in its operation; these then have to be matched to an industry need, otherwise only half the problem has been solved. The transfer of a service into an industry in which it is new can only occur if there is an actual or latent demand for that service. Thus, the marketer of services requires both a broad view and understanding of the service content and of the range of applications within industries in which the service is not familiar.

A whole new profession of systems engineering has emerged precisely to determine how technologies and services can be applied in new ways in industries where they are already used and in industries in which they are unfamiliar. The use of computer techniques in medicine, manpower planning, market model building, and patent search are examples of the organized attempt by a systems engineering approach to seek new markets for an existing technology.

New services for new markets

This clearly is the most difficult situation of all from which to extract profitable new 'product' ideas. It is very much in the 'blue skies' area of planning. For one thing, new ideas for services can arise within an organization or external to it: formally, from R & D and marketing research, informally, via the suggestion box and lunch table discussions. Alternatively, they may be presented to the company as a purchasable opportunity—for example, franchise rights.

It is improbable that ordinary technical people or long-range planners will propose truly visionary or 'blue sky' products. Nevertheless, ideas that are capable of immediate translation into a saleable service and those which have probably only a far off future have their place in a company's planning, and both warrant careful attention.

While it is easy to call for creativity in developing a new service for existing and new markets, it is not possible to achieve it for the asking. So far, the creative process has obstinately resisted analysis and understanding. Its study has been hampered by the problem that it is in motion. Traditionally, the creative process has been considered after the fact—halted for observation which negates the very thing to be studied. The 1960s, however, were years of increasingly intensive study of creativity and the processes which lead to it. The traditional emphasis on sequential logical thinking has certainly not changed, but new developments hold out high hopes for removing creativity from its conventional classification as a 'gift' to that of a skill.

Approaches such as 'lateral thinking'[1] and 'synectics'[2] are opening up ways by which marketing personnel can develop their creative thinking and thus their creative activity capacity in the same way as is occurring with increasing success in the formal sciences.

Although within the narrower definition of this book's subject matter it is a digression to discuss creativity, it is worth while describing one approach —the synectic method—to illustrate how it might be applied to new service development and to marketing as a whole. For the professional service company to be successful, it frequently requires an innovative approach or at least a new combination of conventional inputs.

The word 'synectic' means joining together of different and apparently irrelevant elements to make a whole which is much greater than the parts. The synectic method provides a mechanism by which creative potential can be methodically released and directed at the solution of specific problems— in this case, need identification. Although there are nine phases or steps in the synectic method, in general it makes use of four psychological mechanisms to maintain certain mental states that have been deemed necessary for an individual to be creative. The mechanisms are used to move information that has been stored in the subconscious mind to a conscious level. The four mechanisms are:

1 Personal analogy: identifying with the object or process. This loss of identity allows the individual to assume imaginatively the identity of something inanimate to obtain a new viewpoint of the problem. Alice, faced with the door she could not get through, thought, 'Oh, how I wish I could shut up like a telescope! I think I could, if I only knew where to begin.'

[1] Edward de Bono, *Lateral Thinking*. Ward Lock Educational (London, 1970).
[2] W J Gordon, *Synectics*. Harper & Row (New York, 1961).

2 Direct analogy: this is a comparison between parallel factors in different groups, areas, products, technologies, processes, or activities. 'Where will similar problems to those we are capable of solving exist outside our present areas of activity?' For example, in the field of chemistry, is anything to be learned about desalinization from how a seagull lives in salt water? Consultants, after a study of pricing strategy for a manufacturer of variable chamber filters, recommended that he should segment his market by the cost effectiveness of his product in different applications and obtain a premium price. Would the same method of calculating cost effectiveness as in other multimarket products yield similar results for other firms?

3 Symbolic analogy: this approach uses an image that although technically inaccurate, is aesthetically satisfying as a way of looking at the problem. The individual summons up wordless images or symbols to represent the elements of the problem. They are a unique association of metaphors, complete for the moment, therefore unassailable.

4 Fantasy analogy: this makes the improbable connection between the world as it is and one in which anything is possible as long as it can be imagined. Within this framework, anything is possible and valid, regardless of known natural and physical laws. 'If we used trained ants to represent the microcosm of a population sample, what signals would we need to instruct them into given groupings?'

The employment of these thought procedures during the synectic process produces mental states that are considered necessary for creativity.

- Involvement: a deep interest in the problem and processes used in taking a new look at it which transcends the usual time constraints—persistent thinking, pondering, and dreaming about it.
- Detachment: an ability to get away from looking at the problem in the usual ways.
- Deferment: an ability to withhold acceptance of the first solution—the desire to come up with a unique and elegant solution rather than let time pressures operate to produce only a slight modification of the current solutions.
- Speculation: the recurrent ability to let the mind run free. What would happen if . . . type of questions.
- Autonomy of object: a feeling that the materials or processes under consideration have developed a life of their own, that they possess a separate life, and that they pursue unique relationships independently.[1]

The use of synectics for problem solving on behalf of clients is gaining

[1] This synthesis of the synectic process has been drawn from William J Gordon's book *Synectics*, op. cit. and from *Structured Approaches to Creativity*, a report on the Long Range Planning Service of the Stanford Research Institute (Menlo Park, Calif., 1969).

ground among the more sentient service companies, but few, if any, have considered using it to solve their own service mix and marketing problems.

In so many aspects of marketing, the professional service firm lags a considerable way behind companies concerned with goods or with consumer services. In the development and use of structured approaches to creativity, particularly in relation to new service developments, the opportunity exists to move to the forefront of marketing thought and activity, since all marketers are still on the lower slopes of this development. However, the danger of failing to distinguish between being creative in the abstract and the equally difficult process of being innovative in the concrete is always present. The need for a balance is paramount.

Structuring opportunities for new services

Because the areas of the unknown—market and service—are vast, clearly those services which come somewhere within or close to the company's existing areas of competence and markets should be considered first. In either event, the need for information is paramount. Beginning with a screening or structuring process, it is possible to identify quickly service/market 'packages' on which it is worth spending research money. An example of a first structuring process of service industries, not just professional services, is shown in Figure 13.2. This relates to the search for new service opportunities by an organization skilled in establishing and operating localized services, and seeking to exploit this management and organizational capability. The criteria established for the first screening excluded consideration of any activity with a gambling or gaming element, undertaking, and services linked with the motor industry cycle. These eliminations on one side, any business with an actual or potential market exceeding £10 million was considered. The overview in this case included several professional services, but could as easily have been confined to them. Figure 13.2 shows in broad terms the key factors of:

- market size;
- market growth;
- level of service required;
- competition.

These were then compared with each other and against the firm's criteria for the development of their services and corporate direction and growth. The most suitable services were then isolated and probed in depth. From this probing the marketing and 'product' strategy was developed.[1]

New services searches within all the categorizations described should be a continuing process, as routine as paying salaries. If a systematic procedure is adopted, all the defined areas will be scanned regularly and the findings

[1] A full description of the total structuring process can be found in *Planning a Diversification Strategy*, Industrial Market Research (London, 1970).

recorded. It is important that all new ideas should be classified in accordance with certain of their basic characteristics in order to facilitate the rapid retrieval of those which offer most promise in the light of the special requirements of the firm at any time.

Whether the life cycle of a professional service is a long or short one, it must succumb to the erosion of environmental change and innovation. The need for unremitting search to identify threats to existing services and the way to avert them must be accompanied by the positive, rather than accidental or sporadic, generation of new service ideas and an open-minded approach in the consideration of their introduction.

14

Conclusion

In an era of increasing competition between companies, between services and between technologies, the ability to survive will depend on the adoption of those techniques and approaches which will move the would-be supplier of services or products closer to the user, and this can only be done if a clear understanding is obtained of the user requirements, both those expressed overtly and those desired covertly. But information which is not used intelligently and creatively is of no advantage to those who possess it. While professional service firms have, over the years, sought increasing knowledge and ability in the subject of their professionalism, they have paid scant attention to the means by which they can make their professionalism known and desired. The *laissez-faire* of the older professions, or, at best, their very gentle and gentlemanly ways of making known that they offer a service, has provided a model of practice for the newer consulting professions and services which these have sought to emulate and which has produced an environment as unfortunate for the practitioners as for their clients.

Nicholas Stacey, writing almost 20 years ago on the history of English accountancy, identified as one of the impediments to progress 'the uncombative demeanour of accounting bodies and in turn their members, to many of the contemporary problems which are incapable of solution by reference to existing statutes'.[1] Unquestionably, one of the major problems accountants and other professionals have not yet been able to come to grips with is marketing, because marketing is essentially combative.

The major function of the marketing activities is to present a company's service offering in such a way that prospective clients will perceive values for which they are willing to abandon alternative uses of their money. To

[1] *English Accountancy 1800–1954.* Gee (London, 1954). P. xiii.

accomplish this, the marketing man must recognize the characteristics of his services to which buyers will assign values.

Thus, what is needed is a Janus-like approach—towards the clients and towards the company—to seek to bring as close together as possible client requirements and company output in terms of the needs of supplier and recipient. The closer the integration, the higher the possibilities of the professional service company obtaining continuing satisfactory levels of profitability.

In the final analysis, for all firms' and most institutions' success, whether expressed in terms of an individual's aspirations, job satisfaction, intellectual stimulus, or the opportunity for personal expression and development, it is only profitability which enables the company and individual to continue to operate.

Appendix A

The importance of services in the economy

The original scheme for this book was to have included a chapter which gave a historical summary of the changing economic concepts of 'services' and an overview of the many definitions which have been adopted at various times and in different countries. It was also to provide a quantitative and qualitative background to the consideration of marketing professional services and an economic examination of the importance of services as a whole and of professional services in particular. The final manuscript showed that, while the advocacy in that chapter supported the case for more and better marketing, it interrupted the flow of the narrative and appeared as a divergence to readers wishing to reach the 'how', 'why', 'when', and 'what' of the marketing of professional services. Consequently, the chapter was removed from the main part of the book and now substantially forms this appendix.

Definitions: Official

Definitions of services for official purposes tend to be descriptive rather than delineating the essential nature of the activity. The United Kingdom Central Statistical Office commented: 'If it had been thought necessary to define services it would have been included in *Industrial Classifications—National and International*. It is obvious that services are activities directly relating to the general public—any form of work which is not manufacturing goods.' This definition, to say the least, hardly assists an understanding of what services are.

The Department of Employment and Productivity, which might have been thought to be deeply concerned with definitions, since the categorization of a firm as 'service' or 'manufacturing' governed their liability to Selective Employment Tax, had chosen to use the Standard Industrial Classifications. Thus: 'Activities belonging to orders 1, 2, 20–27 of the SIC, or orders 3–19 but with more than 50 per cent of staff employed on non-production work.' The same procedure is adopted by both the Dutch and Swedish governments.

The Reddaway report, concerned as it was with the effect of the Selective Employment Tax on service trades, and the distributive trade in particular, somehow managed not to define a service even under a heading 'The Nature of Services' and skirted the problem completely.[1]

The United States Department of the Treasury, Internal Revenue Service, describes services as: 'Expenditures which do not result in the acquisition of goods'. This, by definition, excludes the whole area of distribution, utilities, publishing, financial services, and a myriad of other activities.

Definitions: Unofficial

While official definitions give very little guidance to precisely what a service comprises, those developed by economists and others over the years do at least throw some light on the changing concepts of services.

The physiocrats, that remarkable group of eighteenth century French philosophers who believed that the soil provided the only real form of wealth, considered all activities other than agricultural production as services. All other occupations were regarded as if not actually useless, then certainly not particularly laudable.

Adam Smith, who was critical of the physiocratic approach of classifying manufacturing activity, trade, and transportation as sterile, asserted that the material goods production was capable of returning a net income to the producers just as much as agriculture was. However, Smith carefully distinguished between 'productive' and 'unproductive' labour. The provision of services, unlike the labour of manufacture, does not fix and realize itself in some particular subject or vendible commodity which extends beyond the time of the labour involved in its production. The labour was said to be stored up in the product, unlike the labour of a service provider, which perishes at its moment of performance and seldom leaves any trace or value behind it, for which an equal quantity of services could afterwards be procured.[2] Thus, Smith made tangibility, associated with durability of the economic activity, the criterion of productiveness and, consequently, of the distinction between goods and services.

It was, however, J B Say who early in the nineteenth century saw the fallaciousness of Smith's reasoning. J B Say recognized the claims of immaterial wealth alongside those of material wealth and he employed the term 'services' to describe them. The providers of services, he claimed, had the right to be regarded as producers. In fact, it is evident that the term 'services' originated with J B Say in *Traits d'Economie Politique* first published in 1803.

[1] W B Reddaway, *Effects of the Selective Employment Tax. First Report.* HMSO (London, 1970).
[2] Adam Smith, *Wealth of Nations.* Pelican Classics (London, 1970). P. 430.

Alfred Marshall took the concept a step further and narrowed down, once again, what comprised a service. He retained Smith's ideas of perishability implied by the statement that 'man cannot create material things'; thus, productive activities consist of services applied to pre-existing physical materials, but he set out the view which remained current for over half a century when in 1890 in his *Principles of Economics* he wrote:

> It is sometimes said that traders do not produce, that while the cabinet maker produces furniture, the furniture dealer sells what is already produced. But there is no scientific foundation for this distinction. They both produce utilities and neither of them can do more: the furniture dealer moves and re-arranges matters so as to make it more serviceable than it was before and the carpenter does nothing more. The sailor, the railway man who carried coal above ground, produces it just as much as the miner who carried it underground, the dealer in fish helps to move the fish from where it is of comparatively little use to where it is of greater use, and the fisherman does no more.[1]

However, despite the advance in thinking by Marshall, the Smithsonian doctrine continues to apply in many parts of the world, since it became an inherent part of Marxian doctrine which distinguishes, as Smith did, between material and non-material goods and the consequent productiveness or non-productiveness. This is now enshrined in Russian and other Communist countries' national income accounting.

Recent thinking in Westernized countries gave a further dimension to defining services in that the only distinguishing facet between a good and a service is that it does not lead to a change in the form of a good.[2]

Perhaps the most widely accepted current definition, if only to save further argument, is that adopted by the American Marketing Association: 'activities, benefits or satisfactions which are offered for sale'.[3]

What emerges from these changing concepts is a narrowing down of the areas of services—a gradual elimination of functional activities which might, if the process continues, lead to the pure service definition. The position can perhaps best be illustrated as shown in Figure A.1.

It is important to point out the psychologically inferior position of services, not only in Marxian economies, but also in most Western economies. Traditionally, the provision of services was, and still is, regarded as secondary to the production of goods; indeed, the very word 'services' carries the stigma of something menial. The Protestant ethic runs strongly against consumption as opposed to conservation and most particularly against the consumption of immeasurable intangibles, most of which can be associated with luxury,

---

[1] Alfred Marshall, *Principles of Economics*. Vol. 1. (8th ed.) Macmillan (London, 1936) P. 63.

[2] The author is indebted to Professor Harry I Greenfield, Queens College, City University of New York, for the historical summary of the changing concepts of services. It is contained in his book *Manpower and the Growth of Producer Services*. Columbia U P (New York, 1966).

[3] *Marketing Definitions*. American Marketing Association. (Chicago, 1960). P.21.

personal service, self-indulgence, and the satisfaction of psychological and emotional rather than material needs. This attitude is so entrenched that it was even to be found in some of the less thoughtful justifications of the Selectives Employment Tax. Setting aside the fiscal need to bring the purchase of service into line with the purchase of goods, by what standards can it be said that it is more blessed to produce goods than to produce services?

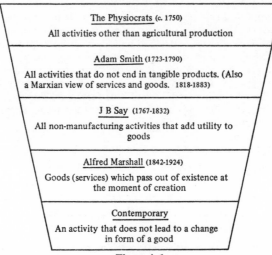

The Physiocrats (c. 1750)

All activities other than agricultural production

Adam Smith (1723-1790)

All activities that do not end in tangible products. (Also a Marxian view of services and goods. 1818-1883)

J B Say (1767-1832)

All non-manufacturing activities that add utility to goods

Alfred Marshall (1842-1924)

Goods (services) which pass out of existence at the moment of creation

Contemporary

An activity that does not lead to a change in form of a good

Figure A.1.

Yet this view applies. Its influence on the marketing of services, even professional services, which are far removed from the pejoratives of 'self-indulgent' and 'luxury', is pervasive and subtle and to counteract it many skills not traditionally associated with service selling, particularly professional services, are required.

Standard Industrial Classification
The obvious, simplest, and least arguable method of classification is to use the Standard Industrial Classification. While it suffers badly from 'absolutism', it leaves little doubt as to whether an activity is a good or a service, but also takes small account of changing technologies and new industrial organization. 'Industries as such have no identity. They are simply classifications of firms which may for the moment be convenient. A change of techniques and/or organization may require a new classification and a new industry.'[1] Alas, the SIC trails a long way behind this desideratum, but nevertheless makes its contribution to an understanding of the differences between goods and services, if only because it is easy to conceptualize an activity. No one has any doubts what happens when metal is welded or goods retailed.

Thus to begin with definitions can be taken by example.

[1] E A G Robinson, *The Structure of Competitive Industry*. Vol. VII. Cambridge Economic Handbooks. Nisbet (London, 1935).

- All economic activities which commence with a pre-existing product and merely change its location (transport) or in a minor way its physical appearance (packaging) or are concerned with its eventual disposition (wholesale and retail trades).
- Banking, real estate, insurance, investment, all provide intangible utilities.
- Recreation, health, law, religion, public administration, accounting, philanthropy, research, and similar activities, are not directly associated with the output of physical commodities and can be included in services.

Two groups, construction and demolition, and utilities, present some borderline problems. Construction and demolition services are more closely allied to goods than services, in that a large part of their output is changing the form of materials: there is ample precedence for categorizing them as goods. Utilities are more difficult to categorize. Worswick and McMahon[1] have stated: 'We have classed them [utilities] as services on the grounds they share most of the qualities by virtue of which services are thought to act as stabilisers' in the economy.

Harry Greenfield expressed an opposite view: 'However, utilities are very much like goods in that they have special, physical characteristics which enable their production to be closely controlled in quantity and quality.'[2]

Perhaps because services have been regarded as a somewhat inferior activity in earlier and current economic thinking, marketers have tended to be defensive in justifying their role in expanding the demand for services. In this respect, their attitude has been not unlike those who market less socially desirable consumer goods, such as some quack medicines, encyclopaedias of dubious educational value, pornography, and addictive drugs. There is little doubt that suppliers of these products meet and satisfy a demand, but the demands are no more respectable than the products or their suppliers. There are, of course, some services that can be classified as socially undesirable, but this is not a reason for marketers of services to be defensive when the very important role which services play in the economies of most countries is under discussion. Certainly, in Britain, it is almost as if there is a conspiracy to make services inferior. The Selective Employment Tax, which was selective only so far as services were concerned, was designed (ostensibly) to encourage labour from unproductive service industries[3] (there was no distinction

[1] C W McMahon and G D N Worswick, 'The Growth of Services in the Economy', *District Bank Review* (London, December 1960). P. 5.

[2] Harry Greenfield, op. cit. P. 19.

[3] 'The Reddaway Report' goes to some length to point out: 'During the course of research, the point has been put to us time and time again that SET has failed miserably in its basic objective of moving labour out of the service trades and become nothing but a device for raising government revenue. We have been left in no doubt that the unpopularity of SET is in large measure accounted for by the widespread impression that SET was "put across" in 1966 *primarily* as a device for moving people out of the service trades and into manufacturing, with its revenue-raising effect kept well out of the limelight. . . .' *Effects of the Selective Employment Tax—The Distributive Trades.* HMSO (London, 1970). P.5.

between strip clubs and stockbroking) to productive (sic) manufacturing industries, and was pejorative by its very nature. The monthly and eagerly awaited balance of payment figures omit invisible earnings of service industries, although in many debit months their inclusion would have shown a total positive balance in the national accounting. As a passing insult, the Queen's Award for Industry was not available to service companies until 1971, and even now is only available for a limited range of services.

Figure A.2 is an interesting exercise originally undertaken by a business journal[1], and shows how the balance of payments in the United Kingdom could look if services were included.

£ million	1964	1965	1966	1967	1968	1969	1970
A. *Visible Trade*							
exports	4466	4777	5122	5042	6143	7018	7728
imports	5003	5042	5214	5576	6807	7141	7872
Visible trade balance	−537	−265	−92	−534	−664	−123	−148
Net adjustment for the recording of exports	+20	+40	+60	+80	+130	+43	+161
Payment for US military aircraft	−2	−12	−41	−98	−109	−61	−10
Visible balance	−519	−237	−73	−552	−643	−141	+3
B. *Invisible Trade*[1]							
exports	2597	2803	2865	3110	3637	4107	4489
imports	2041	2196	2267	2392	2834	3066	3381
Invisible trade balance	+556	+607	+598	+718	+803	+1041	+1108
C. *Private Sectors*							
Overall balance of trade	+37	+370	+525	+166	+160	+900	+1111
D. *Public Sectors*							
Overall balance of trade	−432	−447	−470	−463	−466	−463	−480
CURRENT BALANCE OF PAYMENTS	−395	−77	+55	−297	−306	+437	+631

[1] excludes government services and transfers, but includes public interest, profit and dividends.

Figure A.2. Balance of payments adjusted for invisible trade

It would be as well therefore to examine briefly the role of services in the economy, so that in considering the marketing of professional services the marketer need feel neither defensive nor inferior. Services in their own right make an important, often vital, contribution to the economy and an as yet uncalculated multiplier contribution in terms of improved efficiency throughout industry. This is particularly true of professional services.

[1] *Industry Week* (London, 11 July 1969).

Employment in services

Despite the discouragement and implicit disparagement, there is evidence to show in most industrial countries that services are growing at a faster rate than goods manufacture, certainly in terms of employment; for example, and for the moment ignoring the finer points of classification, this pattern can be seen from the data in Figure A.3.

Stabilizing effects

Perhaps the greatest single contribution of services to the economy is in terms of the stability provided acting as a hedge against the more violent effects of depression.

Four stabilizing effects have been identified:[1]

1 The indivisibility of service output: aeroplanes must fly, even if not full; shops must be staffed, even when not busy; civil servants must be at their posts, even with empty in-trays.
2 The contractual and, therefore, long-term nature of much service activity. Expenditure cannot be easily adjusted to conditions of economic stringency by removing children from a fee-paying school for a term, or by using less of a house to economize on rent for a period. Although margarine can be substituted for butter, it is not plausible or possible to cut down on the 'unseen' distribution costs within the price structure of margarine. Many services, police, education, and medicine, for example, are paid for out of taxes—and these will contract slowly, if at all, in a period of protracted depression.
3 The types of demand which may be said to initiate general fluctuations in the economy are precisely those which affect goods production to a greater degree than the supply of services, for example, exports, government expenditure, investment.
4 It is a basic characteristic of services that they cannot be stockpiled.[2]

Thus, for any or all of these reasons it might be reasonable to assume that the service sector of the economy exercises a stabilizing influence on the economy as a whole, even though some services are highly vulnerable: for example, beauty shops in a town stricken with unemployment, or first class travel facilities and restaurants when firms stipulate rigid expense curtailment.

However, the evaluation of stability deriving from services is not clear-cut. The evidence is strong, but not conclusive. The record of the past 40 years, both in Great Britain and in the United States, shows that in recession or depression service employment has, in fact, been discernibly less subject to decline than manufacturing employment.

---

[1] C W McMahon and G D N Worswick, op. cit.
[2] This statement needs some qualification in the light of the 'concept of tangibility' (see chapter 1).

Changes in the distribution of the working populations of Great Britain, the USA, Germany and the Netherlands between 1960 and 1967.

Country		1960 '000	%	1967 '000	%	Per cent change 1967 as a percentage of 1960
Great Britain	(a)	10 555	45	9 685	40	−8
	(b)	12 837	55	14 755	60	+12
USA	(a)	23 769	35	26 094	34	+11
	(b)	44 375	65	51 252	66	+12
Germany	(a)	13 975	54	12 896	50	−8
	(b)	11 979	46	12 907	50	+7
Netherlands	(a)	1 764	43	1 705	39	−4
	(b)	2 288	57	2 702	61	+18

Sources: *British Annual Abstract of Statistics*, 1968 and *Yearbook of Labour Statistics*, 1968, I L O Geneva.

The civilian workforce, excluding the unemployed, is divided into two categories:

(a) Total engaged in agriculture, forestry, fishing, extraction industries, and manufacturing.
(b) Total engaged in all other types of labour: construction energy, transport, distribution and government, professional and service occupations.

Figure A.3. Employment in service and non-service industries

Productivity

A theory long cherished by economists is that productivity in services compared to goods manufacture does not rise, or rises only slowly, and thus puts a brake on the whole economy. It is difficult at the best of times and in the most propitious circumstances to define and estimate 'productivity'. Certainly, in the service sector, this problem dominates every attempt to make comparisons.

The ostensible reason why productivity in services cannot rise significantly is stated as being the immediacy of services, that is, they are consumed as they are produced and cannot be stockpiled—a view of services which chapter 1 sought to modify. While it is true that the acquisition of one hundred more pairs of scissors without one hundred more barbers will add little to productivity, the accessibility of computer services can materially reduce the time and cost of many operations.

There is ample evidence in the US that service employment has grown, but the increase of output per worker has lagged behind manufacturing industries. Thus, services in the US now employ more than half the country's workers without a parallel rise in the service sector's share of gross national product. Output per service worker increased by only 1.1 per cent from 1929 to 1965 compared with 2.2 per cent average rise for industry, but it has been estimated[1] that only about one-third of the difference was due to a lag in technological change. The gap mostly reflects a lag in capital investment per worker. The improvement in the content of services also contributes to the gap. In other words, output may not have risen but quality has—for example, the ability to solve problems for which solutions exist if firms are willing to spend the money that is necessary to resolve them.

Unquestionably, there have been improvements in major services, such as government and entertainment, which cannot show any growth of output per man. Such 'business', as Fuch points out, presents specially difficult problems of measurement.[2] However, where it has been possible to pinpoint productivity improvements some surprising results have been noted. The largest increases in Britain in productivity in the 1950s were in the gas, electricity, and water utilities, and in public administration and defence. The 'Reddaway Report' contains some detailed and pertinent data on productivity in wholesaling and retailing,[3] showing the same trend.

Thus, the argument that services are not necessarily notably less productive than goods manufacture can be sustained even if they are examined in isolation from their multiplier effect and in terms of added value.

When services are compared with goods in relation to percentage increases in output, the narrowness of the gap is even more obvious.

[1] Victor R Fuch, *The Service Economy*. Columbia U P (New York, 1968). Chapter 3.
[2] Ibid.
[3] 'Reddaway Report', chapters XI, XII and Appendix.

1949 (SIC 1948)

	Sector	Value
S	Gas, etc.	663
S	Insurance, banks	654
S	Distributive trades	558
S	Agriculture	551
S	Transport	519
G	Mining	470
G	Manufacturing	467
S	Various services	449
G	Construction	411
S	Public administration	332
	Goods (less agriculture)	459
	Goods (plus agriculture)	468.5
	Services	478
	Total	**473**

1959 (SIC 1948)

Sector	Value
Gas, etc.	1496
Insurance, banks	1134
Transport	994
Manufacturing	843
Mining	819
Agriculture	816
Distributive trades	811
Construction	800
Various services	731
Public administration	685
Goods (less agriculture)	836
Goods (plus agriculture)	833
Services	828
Total	**830**

1959 (SIC 1958)

Sector	Value
Gas, etc.	1496
Insurance, banks	1134
Transport	992
Manufacturing	861
Mining	817
Agriculture	815
Construction	801
Distributive trades	789
Various services	723
Public administration	687
Goods (less agriculture)	849
Goods (plus agriculture)	846
Services	815.5
Total	**830.5**

1964 (SIC 1958)

Sector	Value
Gas, etc.	2238
Transport	1480
Insurance, banks	1467
Construction	1151
Manufacturing	1117
Mining	1108
Agriculture	1080
Distributive trades	982
Public administration	962
Various services	957
Goods (less agriculture)	1122
Goods (plus agriculture)	1119
Services	1096
Total	**1108**

S denotes Services; G denotes Goods

Figure A.4. UK value added per man in current pounds[1]

[1] G D N Worswick and C G Fane. 'Goods and Services Once Again', *District Bank Review* (London, March 1967).

Figure A.5. Percentage increases in output per man in the UK: average rates per annum over given period[1]

	1949 to 1959				1959 to 1964				
	At current prices	At constant prices		Implicit Price Change	At current prices		At constant prices		Implicit price change
S Gas, etc.	8.5	Gas, etc.	4.0	4.4	Gas, etc.	8.4	Agriculture	6.5	—0·6
S Public administration	8.0	Agriculture	3.6	0.3	Transport	8.3	Gas, etc. }	4.3	3·9
G Construction	6.9	Transport	2.5	4.1	Construction	7.5	Mining	4·2	1.9
S Transport	6.7	Manufacturing	2.3	3.7	Public administration	7.0	Transport	3.3	3.9
G Manufacturing	6.1	Insurance, banks	1.9	3.7	Mining	6.3	Manufacturing	2·0	2.0
G Mining }	5.7	Construction	1.6	5.2	Agriculture }	5.8	Construction	1·6	5.4
S Insurance, banks		Distributive trades	1.3	2.5	Various services		Public administration	1·4	5·5
S Various services	5.0	Various services	1.0	4.0	Manufacturing }	5.3	Distributive trades	1·0	2.
S Agriculture	4.0	Public administration 0.6		7.4	Insurance, banks }		Insurance, banks	1·0	4.1
S Mining	3.8	Mining	0.4	5.3	Distributive trades	4.3	Various services	0·6	5.1
Goods (less agriculture)	6.2		2.1	4.0		5.8		3.2	2.5
Goods (plus agriculture)	5.9		2.2	3.7		5.8		3.4	2.3
Services	5.6		1.6	4.0		6.1		1.8	4.2
Total	5.8		1.9	3.8		5.9		2.7	3.1

S denotes Services; G denotes Goods

[1] Ibid.

There is, however, a further problem which requires consideration in measuring and comparing the productivity of goods and services. The receiver of service often plays an important role in the production of those services which is not paralleled in the production of goods. This unmeasured input can have a significant effect on productivity. The small retailer buying on a cash-and-carry basis accepts the financing and distribution functions of the goods supplier, usually a wholesaler; the manufacturing plant or office building with bulk handling and storage facilities for supplies has accepted the stockholding role of its supplier; facilities for the use of credit transfer methods of payment reduce the accounting work of companies which is then undertaken by the banks. Thus, the degree of sophistication, capitalization, and motivation of the user of services can affect the productivity, and this positive effect is likely to manifest itself in the goods sector rather than the service sector of industry.

All these figures, of course, refer only to enterprises classified as 'services' and do not include manufacturing industries' employment of service personnel. This latter category, as well as mining and agriculture, has been subjected to a long-term trend towards automation. Several Swedish case studies have shown that with the introduction of automation the number of skilled maintenance men on the payroll increased by between 150 and 300 per cent. The growth of high technology in industry has changed employment needs from blue collar towards white collar workers and has upgraded many occupations from skilled to professional status. Growth in the number of white collar workers has also been due to internal factors within corporations, mostly expansion and integration generating the need for increased personnel work and more support and central management services. Similarly, increasing demands of government and other agencies for information and for repayment of taxes and subsidies has of itself created new needs for both internal service personnel and outside professional assistance.

Professional services
These economic factors are primarily considerations for the economist. Within the field of interest of this book the implications of growth in the professional services have one overriding significance: all services professionally rendered, almost without exception, are contributions to productivity in every sector of the economy. Thus, the total level of efficiency of a country's industry as a whole depends in large measure on the provision of the right service at the right time. Value analysis in engineering may save substantial production cost which can easily be lost in less than optimum logistics; brilliant pricing strategies may be negated by poor communications in advertising and selling; financial support, readily, profitably, and efficiently available, is of little use in incorrectly assessed situations. Indeed, there is both a positive and negative multiplier effect in professional services, in that they can so much extend or reduce the reach of the recipient of the service.

That growth in demand for professional services has expanded is unquestionable and reflects both the growing need and confidence of its users.

Service	£M
Advertising	332
Computer services	82
Employment agencies and executive selection	35
Medical and health (private)	33
Management consultancy	25+
Leasing	25
Educational services	16
Consumer marketing research	21
Barristers	10
Solicitors	85
Accountants	60
Architects	32

Figure A.6. Estimated expenditure on selected professional services 1969/70

The volume of business could not have achieved present levels unless it satisfied and continued to satisfy a demand, and unless the users of the services were able to make some evaluation of the benefits they derive from the services.

Economy—as well as convenience—is a major incentive for retaining a professional service firm. The work involved frequently requires a skill that a company cannot afford to employ nor one which they could fully utilize. Service firms, on the other hand, are often able to make large-scale full-time use of highly trained staff and automated equipment to attain great efficiency. They provide economical service by spreading their costs over a group of users.

Several reasons have been ascribed to the growth in demand for professional services:

• The trend towards diversification. Professional services are usually required in a diversification programme both in the development of the programme (R & D, management consultancy, marketing research, production engineering, licence search, patent search) and its implementation. The array of tasks which are secondary to the main occupation of the company are undertaken by outside service companies in order to leave management free to grapple with their major preoccupations.

• Economic, social, technical, and governmental pressures have forced many firms into activities of which they have little experience. These problems may be largely 'one off' or sporadic and lend themselves to the use of external experts, for example for assistance in deciding on the feasibility and choice of a computer installation or the development of a company house style and logos.

- Concentration of industry geographically encourages the development of communal and localized services. These may include security, employment agencies, computer bureaux.
- The range of services themselves has expanded and found new markets which did not previously exist. For example, franchising, factoring, computer time-sharing.

These and other reasons indicate a continuing growth in the demand for and provision of services and, therefore, an intensification of the factors already enumerated, which reveal the beneficial effects on service activity in the economy.

Appendix B

Outline checklist for marketing professional services

1 Strategic considerations

Are the externally imposed or self-imposed restraints on marketing realistic in the light of current conditions? What would be the rewards or penalties for not adhering to them?

Are we fully informed on size, structure, trends, client requirements, competitive climate, and other features of our actual and potential markets? Can we detail them?

Have we defined and agreed our corporate and marketing objectives and expressed them in quantitative terms? Are they available to all concerned as a statement of company policy?

What mix of objectives has been adopted for:

- selling more to existing clients;
- selling existing services to new clients;
- selling new services to old clients;
- selling new services to new clients?

Have we estimated the resources and timespan necessary to achieve our corporate and marketing objectives? Are they detailed?

Have we devised an overall strategy which will achieve the objectives? Is this in written form?

Can the marketing strategy consciously cover more than one reason for purchase? Will more than one strategy be required?

Have we assessed how our markets will change over the next 5 and 10 years, and have we allowed for these changes in our strategy?

Have the individual marketing tasks been defined and assigned?

Is there a written and agreed marketing plan and are all concerned with the marketing of our services familiar with it and with their own role and responsibilities?

Has an evaluation and monitoring system been built into the marketing strategy to permit progress checking?

Have we established criteria for defining our target market (segmentation) and placed a priority order on them? What are they?

Have we assigned the allocation of our marketing resources to the segmentation priorities?

2 The decision-making unit
How many persons must be contacted to close a sale?

- Their job function,
- their names,
- their location?

How many of these people

- do our salesmen visit,
- see our advertising,
- receive our literature?

Through what routes can each of these persons be contacted?

Do we have knowledge of communication between individuals responsible for final decisions and others who contribute towards those decisions?

Are members of decision groups well informed on alternatives available?

Does any method exist of monitoring any changes in the purchasing firm's DMU? If so, what? If not, can one be devised and installed?

Are all the individuals who make a complete assessment and decision fully informed about our service? How do we know?

Is any individual responsible for directing attention of those involved in purchasing to relevant advertisements? Can we identify them?

Who is responsible for drawing up a shortlist of potential suppliers? How accurate is this identification?

Are those concerned in the purchasing process based at the establishment or at head office? To what extent do establishments operate independently?

Is there a formal channel of communication between those holding similar positions in different establishments?

Do committees discuss all factors in the purchasing decision?

Does a mechanism exist for the finance department to be consulted on larger purchases?

To what extent is the board involved in purchasing?

Can the individuals who will consider price against specification be identified? How?

3 Decision-making factors

Have we a method of identifying each buying situation whether it is a:

- new purchase,
- modified new purchase,
- straight rebuy?

What tactics have we devised for each situation?

Can we establish a method for determining which stage in the buy phase an inquiry has reached?

What steps have we taken to formalize our actions to be taken at each stage of the buy phase? How effective are they?

Are the purchasing companies capable of identifying their real needs and of expressing them? If not, how can we assist them?

Are the purchasing companies aware of the full range of services available to meet a particular need, including services competitive to our own?

What are the preferred channels of communication with professional service suppliers?

Should an initial, simpler explanation of the service be aimed at those who would eventually receive the full explanation?

Can those contacted in the purchasing company be relied on to explain the service to the selling company's advantage?

If the facts are requested and given to technical staff, will others to whom they are passed understand them?

Does the information routeing system cut out the important facts at an early stage? If so, how can this be overcome?

Where pure fact-finding functions exist, is information presented in such a way that it can be passed on with minimum effort and loss of material?

Is a purchase of services likely to involve companywide policies?

Is the buying department involved in the purchasing process and consulted at each stage?

Is an old supplier being used because of built-up goodwill, despite being uncompetitive? Is this goodwill a commercial asset?

Is the service concerned purchased in association with some other service or product? If this is the case would the persons considering the other purchase also analyse the service?

What techniques do individuals who consider price against specification use to carry out the evaluation? How does our sales approach and literature fit the evaluation technique?

Are the techniques of value analysis available to those who initiate a project on a price differential? Could we introduce them?

Can purchasing firms be induced or educated to use evaluation methods which favour our services?

Where different individuals are responsible for the purchasing at different price levels, can persons more favourably disposed towards our services be involved in the purchasing decision by a change in the offer price?

Have we identified any innovative content in our offer? Are the salesmen aware of this and capable of expressing it in terms of client benefit? Does our promotion emphasize this innovation?

Are specifications stringent? How far does our service conform to them?

How short should completion times be? Is this more important than adhering to a quoted time, even if longer?

How far ahead does a purchasing company plan?

4 Prospect identification

Do we have full information on our actual and potential markets? If not what steps are we taking to rectify this:

- audit of internal information,
- industrial marketing research?

Has our USP been examined against the needs of the various user segments and individual firms within them?

Are our marketing staff trained to recognize the interface between our services' USP and a client's needs?

Under what circumstances are our services used? Can we identify where and when such circumstances exist beyond our present client classifications?

By what method can marketing staff recognize a potential need for our services?

Does an analysis of our successful bids indicate a method of identifying opportunities among:

- existing clients,
- potential clients,
- emerging potential clients?

Does an analysis of failed bids provide an indication for identifying low level possibilities or for upgrading these possibilities?

Do we know of any contracts which we have not been invited to quote for?

Would an analysis of these situations provide a guide to new business opportunities?

Do we have an environmental monitoring system to identify business prospects as they emerge in response to changed conditions?

Do we have a personnel monitoring system to identify business opportunities arising because of changes in personnel in prospective client firms? If not, can we install one?

Have we assessed how our opportunities for the sale of our services will change over the next 5 and 10 years? What steps have we planned to meet these changes?

5 The selection process

Are specifications drawn in such a way as to allow maximum number of services and companies to be considered?

Is any reference made to official lists provided by professional associations from which names are drawn?

Does a shortlist exist of professional service firms which are invited to tender? Is this shortlist laid down by company policy?

Under what circumstances does the selection of suppliers to quote become limited?

Under what circumstances will this shortlist be altered?

Do financial corporate ties or other links, including infeeding, limit the number of service firms considered?

Is the purchasing strategy designed to ensure that all services are considered despite fixed limitations on the number of suppliers approached?

Which persons limit the number of firms to be considered in a purchasing decision? Have we identified them?

What is the basis for professional service firm evaluation? Is the evaluation systematic?

Was our company considered for inclusion on lists which exist?

Can the reasons for our inclusion or rejection be identified?

What are the characteristics of our competitors or competitors' offers in failed quotation situations?

What are the characteristics of firms who have not invited us to tender?

What are the characteristics of lost business situations?

Are we in possession of sufficient information to make an offer?

Are the reasons why a quotation is being sought understood and is our offer geared to this reason?

Does our offer fully meet the brief?
- Will it, if adopted, reduce uncertainty?
- Does it indicate an understanding of problems?
- Does it demonstrate professionalism?

Has our offer included all the information the DMU will require?

Is our offer unambiguous in all respects? Does it express adequately what the client will receive?

Are the conditions of the offer geared to client needs and does he fully understand commitments he will enter into?

6 The professional service firm
Have we done our S-O-F-T analysis?
- S-trength;
- O-pportunity;
- F-ault;
- T-hreat.

What steps are being taken to exploit or avert these?

Do we have an accurate assessment of all the firm's skills and resources:
- intellectual,
- physical,
- financial,
- markets?

Do we need to develop or acquire more resources? If so, which?

Is our resource allocation comparable with that of competitors? If not, are any differences justified by better performance?

Have we made an assessment of whether our resources are being fully used?

Have we considered the applicability of all the marketing tools? How valid are reasons for rejection of any of them?

What outside influences act on our decisions concerning the use of various marketing techniques and the actual content of marketing?

Are we capable of conducting all the marketing operations or do we need outside assistance in:

- advertising,
- PR,
- marketing research,
- pricing,
- merchandising,
- others (specified)?

At what level of activity would outside purchases of services justify the appointment of internal personnel to undertake them?

Can communications between marketing and professional personnel be improved? If so, how?

Are marketing personnel consulted in price decisions?

Do we have an accurate knowledge of our image among users and non-users of our services? How does it compare to our 'mirror' and 'wish' images and with our competitors?

Does our reputation vary between our different services? Does any such variation imply a change or elimination of some services?

How do we differ from our most successful competitors in:

- size,
- service mix,
- commercial terms,
- marketing methods,
- location,
- length of time established,
- membership of associations,
- prices?

What is the significance of the differences?

What specific advantages do we have over competitors and they over us? Is there any method by which we can increase the former and reduce the latter?

What have been the most successful methods we have adopted in the past for identifying sources of uncertainty? How can they be improved?

What methods can we adopt to demonstrate our professionalism or how can we improve our existing demonstration?

7 Service mix and service development

Does our service have a USP or can we introduce one? Can it be demonstrated?

Do we have a detailed and validated analysis of how our USP fits each market segment?

Which firms could most benefit from the USP of our services?

Have we fully identified them by activity, size, location, or other meaningful criteria, and by name?

Have we considered ways of introducing elements of innovation in our offer? What are they?

Are any reasons for rejecting the introduction of an innovation in our service soundly based on factual evidence?

Is there a high break-cost element in our service which we can exploit? If not, can we develop one?

Does the service purchaser require all the service features?

Can a usable substitute service be developed by a lower cost method?

Could we provide other services and so assist the purchasing company to achieve economies?

Should services be presented as a logical second generation step from the tried and tested service?

Should services be presented as new developments?

Is our product mix the optimum one? What other services do our clients and prospective clients buy which they could purchase from us?

Have we allowed for market changes in our product strategy over the next 5 and 10 years?

Do we have any means of assessing where our services are on their life cycle? What steps are we taking to extend the life cycle or to introduce new services?

Have we given consideration to, and developed a system for, generating new service ideas? What internal organization exists for evaluating, screening, testing, and introducing new service concepts?

Have we listed and evaluated all sources for obtaining new service ideas? Do we have a system for monitoring these sources?

Is our service testable—if so can we use results as a sales platform?

Can we offer a guarantee with our services?

What standards exist for our services and how far do they conform to them?

8 Personal selling

Are market conditions such that personal selling is to be preferred instead of other methods or in conjunction with other methods?

Does our approach to clients' buying personnel correspond with the methods for which preference has been expressed?

Are technical and commercial standards of our salesmen commensurate with buyer requirements?

Do our salesmen understand and sell on the features of intangible marketing:

- reducing uncertainty,
- understanding problems,
- demonstrating professionalism?

Are salesmen motivated to sell by intrinsic methods rather than extrinsic? Do they appreciate the circumstances under which either or both are applicable?

Which method of selling do our salesmen adopt? Is it applicable to:

- persuasion by method,
- persuasion by personnel,
- persuasion by success story?

Are our salesmen's presentations prepared and structured and suitably supported by appropriate sales aids?

Are our salesmen trained and motivated to feed back information from the field? How can they be encouraged in this activity?

Do our salesmen receive support from all our staff, professional and non-professional? If not, why not?

Who is responsible for routeing our salesmen's visits? What is the basis for routeing? Is it effective?

Should salesmen call at establishments as well as head offices?

Should the ground have been prepared by other methods prior to our salesman's visit? If so, in which way?

Are the personnel our salesmen normally see influential in the purchasing decision? On whose assessment is this opinion based?

Are our salesmen diverted to non-important individuals?

Are salesmen normally able to obtain access to individuals who influence the buying decision? If not, how can they be assisted to reach the decision-makers?

Can our salesmen present a valid and acceptable reason to the person deputed to handle the inquiry for wanting to see other members of the staff?

Can methods be developed, such as conferences or technical symposia, which will enable salesmen to obtain access to individuals in the buying firm they would like to see but who are not normally available to them?

What other methods of sales promotion are needed to reach the personnel whom the salesmen cannot see?

9 Sales promotion

Who are the major audiences for our promotion, and what are the media and methods by which we can reach them?

Are our promotional objectives clear and accepted by all concerned?

What is the route to their attainment?

Does our promotional material emphasize client benefit and satisfaction or is it entirely extrinsic?

Is our promotional material understandable to non-experts? Does it carry conviction of the type which will reduce uncertainty? Has it been tested?

Is our method for appropriation setting formal and understood by all our marketing personnel? Is it consistently applied?

Have all methods of promotion been evaluated as to their suitability and likely effectiveness?

What are the reasons for rejecting any promotional techniques?

Have they been rigorously and objectively scrutinized? Do they reflect historic reasons or in-built prejudice?

Is press advertising appropriate for our service and under what circumstances?

Would any advantages occur if advertising were more/less regionalized? What would they be?

Do we know if literature is being received by those who want and use it?

If brochures and other literature are routed through purchasing officers, what methods can be developed to ensure they reach others whose decision in a buying situation is important?

Is direct mail a suitable technique for our service? If not, why not and are the reasons for rejection soundly based?

Should direct mail be addressed to establishments or head offices to reach those involved in the purchasing decision?

Is direct mail correctly addressed to interested persons within the prospect company?

Under what circumstances would PR be preferable to press advertising? When should they augment each other?

Are PR targets clearly specified and understood? Does a method exist for assessing if and when they have been achieved?

Can we merchandise our service? If so, in what manner?

Does a measure exist of evaluating the success of promotion strategies?

10 Pricing
Are we adhering to a fixed or accepted price policy?

Have we assessed the implications of departing from such a system? What would be the advantages and disadvantages?

Have we a pricing strategy? If so, is it compatible with our marketing and corporate strategy? If not, can a pricing strategy be developed?

Does our costing system provide a reliable base for price setting?

What methods exist to check the efficiency of our costing methods?

What methods of pricing have been considered and what reasons have been advanced for not adopting them? Conversely, why has the method chosen been selected?

- Cost pricing;
- Competitive pay pricing;
- Contingency payment pricing;
- Fixed price;
- Contract pricing;
- Value pricing;
- Others.

What price tactics have we considered and what reasons have been advanced for not adopting them? Conversely, why has the current method been selected?

What methods do we use to arrive at price in competitive bidding situations? How successful are these?

What alternative methods have been considered for deciding price in a competitive bidding situation?

Bibliography

There is no bibliography as such on the marketing of professional services, and barely any on marketing any other service. Thus, for further reading, it is necessary to piece together relevant sections of a wide range of books concerned with marketing functions and with the professions. The following list is a representative selection of specialist books covering broad marketing functions, and also books in which sections will be found which are directly applicable to professional service marketing.

Marketing

R S Alexander, J S Cross, and R M Cunningham. *Industrial Marketing*. Irwin (Homewood, Ill., 1956).

P D Converse, H W Huegy, and R W Mitchell. *Elements of Marketing*. Prentice-Hall (Englewood Cliffs, N J, 7th Ed, 1965).

H R Dodge. *Industrial Marketing*. McGraw-Hill (New York, 1970).

M S Heidingsfield. *Changing Patterns in Marketing—A Study in Strategy*. Allyn & Bacon (Boston, Mass., 1968).

L H Hodges and R Tillman. *Bank Marketing*. Addison-Wesley (Reading, Mass., 1968).

E J Kelley. *Marketing Strategy and Functions*. Prentice-Hall (Englewood Cliffs, N J, 1965).

Theodore Levitt. *Innovation in Marketing*. Pan Books (London, 1968).

Theodore Levitt. *The Marketing Mode*. McGraw-Hill (New York, 1969).

J G Matthews, R D Buzzell, T Levitt, and R E Frank. *Marketing—An Introductory Analysis*. McGraw-Hill (New York, 1964).

E C Miller. *Marketing Planning*. American Management Association (New York, 1968).

D D Parker. *The Marketing of Consumer Services*. University of Washington (Seattle, 1960).

Leslie Rodger. *Marketing in a Competitive Economy*. Associated Business Programmes (London, 1971).

S R Simon. *Managing Marketing Profitably*. American Management Association (New York, 1969).

Aubrey Wilson. *The Art and Practice of Marketing*. Hutchinson (London, 1971).

Aubrey Wilson, ed. *The Marketing of Industrial Products*. Pan Books (London, 1972).

John Winkler. *The Annual Marketing Plan*. Associated Business Programmes. (London, 1972).

John Winkler. *Marketing for the Developing Company*. Hutchinson (London, 1969).

Professional practices

F. A. R. Bennion. *Professional Ethics*. Charles Knight (London, 1969).

A M Carr-Saunders and P A Wilson. *The Professions*. Cass (London 1964).

G Millerson. *The Qualifying Associations*. Routledge & Kegan Paul (London, 1964).

W J Reader. *Professional Men*. Weidenfeld & Nicholson (London, 1966).

The Monopolies Commission. *Professional Services*. HMSO (London, 1970).

Planning

H Igor Ansoff. *Corporate Strategy*. Penguin (London, 1968).

S C Blumenthal. *Management Information Systems: A Framework for Planning and Development*. Prentice-Hall (Englewood Cliffs, N J, 1969).

D W Ewing. *The Practice of Planning*. Harper & Row (New York, 1968).

P Hilton. *Planning Corporate Growth and Diversification*. McGraw-Hill (New York, 1970).

E P Learned, C R Christensen, K R Andrews, and W D Guth. *Business Policy —Texts and Cases*. Irwin (Homewood, Ill., 1969).

Selecting a service company

W C Gordon Jr. *Selecting Marketing Research Services*. Small Business Administration (Washington DC, 1960).

How to Control the Quality of Management Consulting Engagements. Association of Consulting Management Enterprises (New York, March 1970).

How to Get the Best Results From Management Consultants. Association of Consulting Management Engineers (New York, 1964).

Manual of the Use of Consultants in Developing Countries. United Nations (New York, 1968).

Purchasing

Theodore Levitt. *Industrial Purchasing Behaviour*. Graduate School of Business Administration. Harvard University (Cambridge, Mass., 1965).
P J Robinson, C W Faris, and Y Wind. *Industrial Buying and Creative Marketing*. Allyn & Bacon (Boston, Mass., 1967).
A E Smith. *New Techniques for Creative Purchasing*. Dartnell (Chicago, 1966).
How British Industry Buys. Hutchinson (London, 1967).

Creativity

E de Bono. *Lateral Thinking*. Ward Lock Educational (London, 1970).
W J C Gordon. *Synectics*. Harper & Row (New York, 1961).
S J Parnes and H F Harding, eds. *A Source Book for Creative Thinking*. Charles Cribner (New York, 1962).

Marketing research

P E Green and R E Frank. *A Manager's Guide to Marketing Research*. Wiley (New York, 1967).
M S Heidingsfield and F H Eby. *Marketing and Business Research*. Holt, Rinehart & Winston (New York, 1962).
E Konrad and R Erickson. *Marketing Research—A Management Overview*. American Management Association (New York, 1966).
J R Rummel and W C Ballaine. *Research Methodology in Business*. Harper & Row (New York, 1963).
Aubrey Wilson. *The Assessment of Industrial Markets*. Hutchinson (London, 1968).

Personal selling

R V Butt. *Sales Effort and Marketing Strategy*. American Management Association (New York, 1969).
M Hanan, J Cribbin, and H Heiser. *Consultative Selling*. American Management Association (New York, 1970).
E Hodnett. *Effective Presentations*. Parker (West Nyack, New York, 1967).
D Rowe and I Alexander. *Selling Industrial Products*. Hutchinson (London, 1968).

Advertising

D B Lucas and S H Britt. *Measuring Advertising Effectiveness*. McGraw-Hill (New York, 1963).
F R Messner. *Industrial Advertising*. McGraw-Hill (New York, 1963).
Papers for the Seminar on Measuring Advertising Effectiveness. European Society for Opinion Surveys and Market Research (Munich, 1–13 April 1965).

Public relations
J Derriman. *Public Relations in Business Management.* University of London Press (London, 1964).
J W Riley, ed. *The Corporation and Its Publics.* Wiley (New York, 1963).

Merchandising
A Gillam. *Commercial Merchandising.* UKCTA (London, 1969).
D B Wright. *Principles of Merchandising.* Butterworth (London, 1969).

Pricing
W Brown and E Jacques. *Product Analysis Pricing.* Heinemann (London, 1964).
R A Lynn. *Price Policies and Marketing Management.* Irwin (Homewood, Ill., 1967).
A R Oxenfeldt. *Pricing for Marketing Executives.* Wadsworth (Belmont, Calif., 1966).
E Marting, ed. *Creative Pricing.* American Management Association (New York, 1968).

The service economy
V R Fuch. *The Service Economy.* Columbia U P (New York, 1968).
H I Greenfield. *Manpower and the Growth of Producer Services.* Columbia U P (New York, 1966).
S Kuznetz. *Modern Economic Growth.* Yale U P (New Haven, Conn., 1969).
W B Reddaway. *Effects of the Selective Employment Tax: First Report.* HMSO (London, 1970).
Britain's Invisible Earnings. British National Export Council (Pitman, London, 1966).

Author index

Subject index

Competitive variables, 88
Computers and computing services, 6, 7, 11, 18, 21, 37, 79, 90, 137, 148, 150, 169, 170
Consultant professions, 5, 82, 131
    ethics of the, 4, 15–18, 82–84, 111, 119, 131
Consultative services, defined, 3
Consulting engineers, 8, 11, 28, 36, 42, 82, 83, 97, 130, 137, 148
Consumer services (*see also* Services)—
    classified, 6–10
    defined, xi, 2, 5
    distinguished from producer services, 5–10
Contingency payment pricing, 134, 181
Continuous market feedback, 20, 89, 108, 179
Contract pricing, 135, 181
Contract R & D services, xii, 6, 8, 9, 11, 28, 58, 83, 91, 113, 129, 130, 169
Corporate long-range planning, 66, 67, 75, 78, 81, 104, 110, 129, 130
Cost control, 92–94, 132, 133
Cost effectiveness, 55, 97, 106, 108, 152
Cost pricing, 134, 181
Costing, 132, 133
Creative process, the, 35, 36, 116, 117, 146, 151–153
    mental states in, 151, 152
Credit strategies, 14, 70
Critical path analysis, 49
Current image, 121, 122
Customer behaviour, analysis of, 17, 19, 89, 97, 98
Customer variables, 88

Decision-makers and the decision-making unit (DMU), 37, 41, 42, 52, 58, 61, 63, 69, 79, 80, 99, 105, 136, 137, 172, 173
Decision-making process, 63, 104, 173, 174
Demonstration of professionalism, 27, 31–33, 63, 65, 69, 70, 100, 108, 138, 176, 177, 179
Differentiated advantages, 19, 89
Differentiated marketing, 19, 89
Direct mail advertising, xiii, 19, 70, 87, 114, 123–127, 180, 181
    monitoring lists for, 124
    objectives of, 126, 127
    sources of information for, 124
Discount pricing, 136, 137
Discrete pricing, 136, 137
Diversionary pricing, 136, 137
Durability concept, 6–8, 11

Employment agencies, *see* Executive search companies

Employment in service and non-service industries, 163, 164
Environmental variables, 88
Equipment services, defined, 2
Essentiality concept, 6, 10
Estate agents and auctioneers, 6, 8, 131
Ethics of the consultant professions, 4, 15–18, 82–84, 111, 119, 131
Executive search companies, and employment agencies, 6, 8, 12, 21, 42, 103, 129, 130, 134, 148, 169, 170
Exhibitions and demonstrations, 14, 70, 115, 119, 123
Extrinsic approach to selling, 30, 32, 44, 65, 66, 68–70, 100, 101, 104, 105, 179

Facilitating services, defined, 3
Factors and factoring services, 6, 8, 9, 53, 67, 68, 114, 129, 169, 170
Fixed pricing, 131, 132, 134, 181
Follow-through procedure, 109
Franchise dealings, 8, 14, 53, 151, 170

Generic definition of services, 18, 89
Go no-go procedure, 49, 50
Goods, *see* Products
Guarantee pricing, 136, 137
Guarantees, provision of, 14, 22, 68, 70, 178

Human engineering, 148

Identification of professionalism, 27, 31–33, 63, 65, 69, 100, 108, 138, 176, 179
Identifying market opportunities, *see* Market opportunities, identification of
Identifying prospects, *see* Prospect identification
Image, the, 47, 87, 118–124, 126, 138, 143, 144, 177
    current, 121, 122
    mirror, 121, 122, 177
    optimum, 121, 122
    wish, 121, 122, 177
Industrial services, *see* Producer services
Industrial Training Boards, 55, 62
Industry relations, 120
Information retrieval systems, 45, 90, 92, 106, 129
Innovation, 149, 151, 153, 154, 178
Innovative content, 57, 58, 61, 140, 174
Institute of Journalists, 4
Institute of Marketing, 43, 44
Institution of Mechanical Engineers, 43
Institute of Public Relations, 119
Insurance, 6, 8, 9, 11, 19, 26, 37, 38, 53, 54, 57, 91, 97, 113, 125, 127, 129–131, 137, 143, 161, 166, 167

Printed in Great Britain by A. Wheaton & Co. Ltd., Exeter